SPEED
NO INT'L AIRPORT

LIFE OF THE LAND

Articulations of a Native Writer

Dana Naone Hall

'AI PŌHAKU

PAGE I

Dana Naone Hall responds to the support of passing motorists along Ka'ahumanu Avenue in Kahului.

Photograph by Masako Cordray.

FRONTISPIECE [PAGE II]

Ho'okipa. In the distance is Mauna Kahalawai (the West Maui Mountains).

Photograph by Dana Naone Hall.

The kapa pattern reproduced on page iii and throughout the book is based on a kapa piece created by Puanani Van Dorpe.

The author thanks the following publications in which the poems within this volume first appeared, some in slightly different form:
Ho'omānoa, *Honolulu Star-Bulletin*, *Kaimana*, *Mālama Hawaiian Land and Water*, *'Ōlelo Hou*, *Telescope*

Special thanks to Barbara Pope, Maureen Liu-Brower, Elizabeth Lee, and Malia Hitch for their help in making this book.

PUBLISHED BY 'AI PŌHAKU PRESS
Distributed by:
Native Books/Nā Mea Hawai'i
P. O. Box 3080
Honolulu, Hawai'i 96802
info@nameahawaii.com
www.nameahawaii.com
808-596-8885

LCCN 2016958242
ISBN 978-1-883-52844-7

Designed and produced by Barbara Pope Book Design, Honolulu
Printed and bound in the United States

For Isaac and Leahi

and
Ka Poʻe Hawaiʻi
precious and numerous
as grains of sand

CONTENTS

ʻŌlelo Mua

Ua mau ke ea o ka ʻāina i ka pono. Most know this to be the Hawaiʻi state motto, which officially translates as "The life of the land is perpetuated in righteousness." King Kamehameha III, Kauikeaouli, first uttered the phrase on July 31, 1843, at the end of an illegal British occupation of the Hawaiian Kingdom; in this context, the saying's meaning was "The sovereignty of the land continues as is just." While both interpretations touch on sentiments expressed in the statement, they do so in tension: a poetic declaration of US incorporation runs counter to the unrelinquished claim of Hawaiian independence. When very different assertions of nationhood clash in the same space, how can the land live sovereign through words and actions that are pono (good, just, righteous, balanced)?

Fortunately, Dana Naone Hall has mapped out a path for us in this critical volume containing a wide range of her writings from over the last thirty-plus years—poetry, public talks, legal testimonies, official letters, newspaper editorials, interview excerpts, and scholarly essays. One of Maui's most tireless advocates, Dana shows how imagination, commitment, labor, and love perpetuate the ea (sovereignty and life) of the land that we, who are fortunate enough to call Hawaiʻi home, live in.

Dana, originally from Kāne'ohe, is a Kamehameha Schools and University of Hawai'i graduate, as well as a nationally recognized poet. She started teaching in Hawai'i public schools in the early 1970s. Dana became active in Native Hawaiian and environmental issues in 1984, when she, her husband Isaac Hall (a water and land use attorney), and families from Mākena (in the Honua'ula district of South Maui) formed the Hui Alanui o Mākena to prevent Seibu Hawaii (which was building the Maui Prince Hotel) from closing the old Mākena Road that ran along the path of the ancient Alaloa established by Kihaapi'ilani, a thoroughfare also known as the "King's Highway" or "Pi'ilani Trail." Such a closure would have denied Native Hawaiians access not only to the resources of the ocean but also to an essential source of their ancestral identity— the trail itself. A protracted three-year battle led to the settlement detailed in this book ("A Poetry of Place"). Seibu also agreed to not support any further closures of the coastal road at Palauea, which later helped the Hui Alanui o Mākena and others secure over 20 acres of land for a cultural preserve. It was "99 percent trench work" (Dana's definition of activism, spelled out in her introduction) that won these gains. We see just a fraction of this work in Dana's writings, which describe both the early and the ongoing efforts to bring about a new era for Honua'ula (including Wailea and Kaho'olawe, which also receive attention here). As she says in "Palauea Preserve," this is a place where "a sovereign wind blows."

The trail from Mākena led to the struggle at Honokahua in West Maui. Over a thousand iwi kupuna were disinterred there before Hawaiians from across the islands came to Maui to oppose the desecration. Many then gathered at the state capitol to further voice their resistance, which resulted in the preservation of the burial site and the relocation of the Ritz-Carlton hotel. More important, this led to the birth of the Native Hawaiian burial movement and the formation of Hui Mālama I Nā Kūpuna o Hawai'i Nei. It was also the basis for amending the state's historic preservation law to include new protections for Native Hawaiian burial sites and to establish island burial councils (IBCs) for Hawai'i, Maui/Lāna'i, Moloka'i, O'ahu, and Kaua'i/Ni'ihau. Dana would serve as chair and vice chair of the Maui/Lāna'i Island Burial Council, which has arguably been one of the most effective IBCs in the state. In "Pa'a Ke Kahua," she recounts the early days of this struggle and reminds us all that, as its name suggests, Honokahua serves as "the foundation from which we can continue to grow and thrive as a people."

My own path on this journey began in 1995 when I was a junior in college in snowy New Hampshire, writing a paper for an environmental studies project. On my mother's recommendation, I called Dana to get a sense of the major cultural and environmental issues facing our home island of Maui. One thing led to another, and the following summer I interned for Dana while she and Isaac were fighting the State Department of Transportation's efforts to extend the Kahului Airport runway to allow the landing of larger aircraft carrying tourists from much greater distances than before. Days spent combing through hundreds of pages of a woefully inadequate Draft Environmental Impact Statement were counterbalanced with visits to a burial site near the proposed airport expansion and the nearby Kanahā wetland habitat of the endangered ae'o (Hawaiian stilt). The reverence and beauty of the latter stood in stark contrast to the shortcomings of the former, and Dana's guidance led me to a new kind of seeing—of what was there (in the land) and what was missing (in the plans).

With this knowledge came a revelation from my grandmother and her sister that our family had traditionally been caretakers of the burials at Pi'ihana and Waiehu; sand mining threatened both locations (Dana writes about this in "Archaeological Conference Talk"). Dana also taught me that we need to take advantage of every opportunity we have to speak for the kūpuna (ancestors) and the plains in which their bones are planted. By doing so we ensure that "the life of this land will continue to be perpetuated for future generations," as she says in "Every Day Is Earth Day."

This book will hold wide appeal to all who, like Dana, have "an abiding interest in continuity and the possibilities of reconnection" ("The Road to Cultural Justice"). Students and community members interested in environmental stewardship, responsible development, historic preservation, burial protection, applied archaeology, language revitalization, federal recognition, Hawaiian sovereignty, and contemporary poetry will gain much from these pages. When speaking with Dana about the collection, she described it as "less a text and more a companion to those engaged in the struggle, those who want to become more familiar with the issues, and those who love Hawai'i." Her goal in writing was "to inspire others by actions to wake up, or simply remind them of the beauty that surrounds us and the necessity of doing something to preserve it."

It is perhaps no coincidence that the Hawaiian word for "awaken" is *ala*—which also means "path, road, trail." The continuity that Dana speaks of in "The Road to Cultural Justice" and in other writings throughout the book refers not only to the sustained presence of the Kanaka 'Ōiwi (Native Hawaiians) on and in the land but also to the continued vigilance required to ensure that the sands of our shores remain as final resting sites and future birthplaces for all who pursue justice and righteousness in the islands. This is pono in practice—an art and an ethos exemplified in Dana's words throughout this volume. "If you do not see," to quote from her concluding poem, "Keone'ō'io Fishpond," then "Look again."

Ty P. Kāwika Tengan

Associate Professor, Departments of Ethnic Studies and Anthropology
University of Hawai'i at Mānoa

Preface

In the temporal world of Hawaiʻi politics, change is the one constant. Sometimes the change occurs over a long period of time, as with the budding, then blossoming, awareness of the unextinguished sovereignty of Kanaka ʻŌiwi. At other times the changes happen rapidly, as in the last two years when successive, and sometimes unexpected, events have fueled the debate about which model of sovereignty to choose—the creation of an independent nation or federal recognition, affording a government-to-government relationship with the United States.

Creating a government is a difficult and complex process that requires the informed participation of those to be governed. However, Hawaiʻi is unique in that a growing body of Native Hawaiian law has developed over the last four decades. The recognition of traditional and customary rights, and the adoption of one of the strongest burial protection laws to be found anywhere, among other statutes and provisions of benefit to Native Hawaiians, form a part of the foundation for the sovereign entity that will come next.

Much of the writing in this book is about engaging with government—in the spirit of the poetic, oratorical, and testimonial traditions of our people.

Putting a Love of Reading and Writing to Work—An Introduction I

Nestled on the left side of my mother (my brothers occupied the other side) on the pūneʻe in our living room, I listen to my mother's beautiful, expressive voice read to us about the adventures of Br'er Rabbit, who outwitted the Fox, and the tale of Little Black Sambo, the boy who saved himself from being eaten by tigers, with its marvelous ending of the tigers chasing each other until they turned to butter. Or, perhaps my favorite, the story of the great, pacific, flower-smelling Spanish bull, Ferdinand.

Early attempts to teach me to read at school were met with puzzlement on my part. I could not understand who Dick and Jane might be, and no dog I knew was called Spot. Despite this initial hurdle, I must have figured it out, for I have been happily lost and found in reading ever since.

I remember writing for the pleasure it brought me to fashion a graceful line, and to convey something beyond the words and the subject at hand, in high school. A tenth-grade English teacher encouraged me to join the school newspaper staff, which provided me with a means to create a little island on which I could survive the tempests of the next two years.

Freed from the strictures of secondary school, and accepted at the University of Hawaiʻi at Mānoa, I jumped into the ocean. Literally. I spent far more time on the sands of Ala Moana and Queen's Surf than I did in any classroom at the university that year. Often I showed up for one or two sessions at the beginning and was never seen again for the remainder of the semester.

The one exception was my freshman English class. Here I was introduced to a metaphoric reading of *The Autobiography of Malcolm X* and was loaned a copy of James Wright's *The Branch Will Not Break*—a slim volume of contemporary American poetry, which opened up a new way of seeing and writing about the world.

More than anything, my reading of contemporary poetry inspired my own efforts. Just in time to show up with a small sheaf of poems at the door of a professor who would judge if I would be allowed into the department's first poetry workshop.

My engagement with poetry mushroomed. In addition to writing, I edited the first issues of the university's literary magazine, *Hawaii Review* and helped organize readings for visiting writers such as Robert Bly, John Logan, and W. S. Merwin.

Before I left the university, I began teaching poetry part-time in the public schools with the Poets-in-the-Schools program. For the next thirteen years I taught at several schools a year, beginning on Oʻahu then continuing on Maui when I moved there.

It took seven years of watching the political scene on Maui from a distance and muttering with friends about the current state of affairs before I managed to squeeze out a little article on ʻOhana Makaʻala (a one-man leafleting campaign in Waikīkī asking tourists to go home until Hawaiʻi could solve its problems), causing my soon-to-be-husband Isaac Hall to laugh at my naïveté. I learned quickly.

One of the things I learned is that activism consists of 99 percent trench work. Working with groups like Hui Alanui o Mākena and Maui Mālama Pono made the effort less onerous—and often even fun, as we spent time together in places that we loved and wanted to protect.

In speaking on behalf of these special places, I sought to leaven polemical language with poetic expressions of aloha ʻāina. I also wanted to convey as much pertinent information as possible to aid those in decision-making positions. Often this meant reading and analyzing hundreds of pages of documents and having some familiarity with the relevant law, as evidenced by the Brescia Case and Kawaiahaʻo Multi-Purpose Center letters.

This book contains a selection of work from 1984 to the present. Some of the writing concerns long-term campaigns like the ones waged over Honokahua, Kahului Airport, and Waiheʻe. Other pieces involve one-time opportunities. From broad perspectives to nearly microscopic details, these selections indicate the range of political engagement possible.

Over time the love of reading and writing became a practice—a way of contributing, with others, to the life of this land.

Maui, Hawaiʻi
2016

Local Poetry and the Making of an Activist

2

PRESENTATION TO THE KIWANIS CLUB OF MAUI
APRIL 18, 1991

When I awoke this morning it was raining, and it reminded me of where I grew up in Kāneʻohe, on the windward side of the island of Oʻahu.

Generally, the talks I give are centered on political issues, which are also by nature cultural issues, but before I speak more directly about politics I'd like to take you back for a few moments to Kāne-ʻohe, to describe a small green world that exists now only in the imagination.

Kāneʻohe was a very small rural town when I was growing up. In traditional times, often referred to as prehistory, Kāneʻohe was one of nine ahupuaʻa (a traditional division of land) that lined Kāneʻohe Bay. Numerous freshwater springs attesting to the presence of Kāne, god of the life-giving waters, fed the taro patches and nurtured the fisheries of the bay. Driving along the Windward Coast, it is still possible to see the remnants of fishponds, called loko iʻa. Kāneʻohe was a complete world for Hawaiians and sustained one of the largest populations on the island.

Leaping forward some hundreds of years, my own memories of the place have survived fires that burned down the original wood frame buildings of the elementary school I attended—the year after

I graduated from high school. And my family's first house, after we no longer lived in it, burned to the ground four years later on the Fourth of July. Two childhood landmarks disappeared in the same way.

But, in memory, I still walk the half mile or so between the school and our house on the hill. Past the fire station directly across the street from the school and farther along, the big lipstick tree shading a curve of Paleka Road. Past croton hedges and the neighborhood dogs, and the mostly green- or white-painted wooden houses set back behind plumeria trees. Closer to home, the familiar house of one of my father's sisters (who was named Humuʻula after a boat that shuttled Big Island cattle to Honolulu in the early years of the century), her house spilling over with six daughters.

Then the well-tended yard of Mr. Holt, who won a Hicks home in a sweepstakes one year. Everyone looked on in awe as it was being built, the visible signs of his good fortune assembled in full view of the neighborhood.

On the last corner, the coconut trees I gazed down on from our house and thought of as anchoring in some way the whole known landscape. After I was already grown, one of the tallest trees was cut down by a local tree trimmer. The tree exacted its revenge when we heard the tree trimmer's scream in the middle of dinner. He was saved by his safety harness.

At the base of the hill was Mrs. Centeio's garden and the smell of pasteles steaming in her kitchen. In the years to come her garden would be taken over by an Okinawan man, who was very kind but grew lemons almost too sour for anything.

If you were to follow the narrow road that wound past our house, you would arrive at a Filipino camp shaded by mango trees and java plums. In 1962 a bulldozer scraped that part of the world away, and in its place appeared paved streets along with rows of houses and their collections of cars, fences and handkerchief-sized lawns. Even the stream, which once followed its own course through that vanished landscape, was made to flow along a concrete ditch to keep it from flooding the bordering properties during heavy rains. Only the steep-sided green slopes of the Koʻolau mountains behind the town bridged both worlds.

As a child there doesn't seem to be much that one can do to prevent the destruction of familiar places, but after moving to Maui fourteen years ago I found myself witnessing all over again the destruction of a rural place. The difference is that this time I feel that I can do something about it.

I am reminded of a statement from a talk that Maurice Myers, the chairman of the Hawaii Visitors Bureau and the chief executive officer of Aloha Airlines, gave last month on Maui. He said, "And we all know that real life in Hawaiʻi revolves around tourism."

That's the same prejudiced, canted view that terms the overdevelopment of the islands as growth, followed by the admonition: You can't stop progress. From my perspective, what we are witnessing and participating in is not growth or progress so much as it is outright destruction. Or to put it another way, the growth of destruction.

As a Hawaiian I have to be concerned about the destruction of Hawaiʻi, and because I live here I am particularly concerned about the destruction of Maui.

We have a number of enlightened laws on the books dealing with Native Hawaiian access rights and water rights. However, the interpretation of these rights and the actual exercise of these rights and their application have proven to be less straightforward.

I often find myself in direct conflict with government entities that seem to be working assiduously on behalf of prodevelopment forces, adopting what are called "mitigation plans" for development projects that trivialize the concerns and needs of the local, resident population.

As Kekuni Blaisdell, a medical doctor and former director of the Center for Hawaiian Studies at the University of Hawaiʻi at Mānoa, put it: "Closed government is more than a question of access to documents." He also said:

> My concern is the attitude shown by government agencies toward Native Hawaiians. We have to correct this mentality, that "you Native Hawaiians are just like everybody else." In Hawai'i we are the native people and the government has recognized this, but refuses to really act upon it. All we ask is the respect that should be given to indigenous people, for our culture, language, religion, health and survival in our native land. No more and no less. (Panel, March 17, 1988)

In the dominant Western culture of Hawai'i today, the paramount rights appear to be property rights. Some contentious cases involve conflicting property rights: the construction of a building that would block a neighbor's view of the ocean, for instance. Individual members of the public and citizen advocacy groups are often left alone in the struggle for public rights. We have only to drive along the coast where the major resorts are located on Maui to determine which side prevailed in the battle for beach and ocean access rights.

But poor planning and decision-making in the past need not be the seedbed for more of the same in the future. The Maui County Council is presently considering a moratorium on further hotel development until the physical infrastructure can be brought up to par, if you will excuse the golf term. The council is not seriously contemplating bringing the social infrastructure up to par—human services are always underfunded and understaffed. We might say roads and sewers first, women and children last.

Despite council talk of a moratorium, Alexander & Baldwin wants to build a 150-suite hotel in an area that is not designated for resort development—Pā'ia, a small, rural, lately-cum-windsurfer town. It is one of my hopes that before every accessible place on Maui is paved over and remade in the image of somewhere else, stringent planning policies will be instituted designating areas that are inappropriate for certain kinds of—or in some cases any—development.

A Pā'ia with a shopping mall and an all-suite hotel will not be the Pā'ia of the fifth grader who wrote the following poem:

FISHING AT PAIA

Waves crash against the rocks
Making a loud roaring sound.
I can see the fish stealing
and eating my bait happily.
Then suddenly

I see my father's ulua pole
bending like a coconut tree in the strong wind.
As my father reels it in
I can see a dark shadow coming in.
It is a twenty-one-inch ulua.
On shore it flaps around
like a wounded bird.
Its top half is full of glittering spots
and the bottom half is as blue as the sky.
Just before the tail
there are three little bumps.
As I look closer I can see the bumps
As shark fins cutting through the water.
When I am about to put my line in the water,
there is no fish in sight.
There is only black rocks
with green seaweed swaying back and forth.
Then after my line is in
the fish suddenly appear again.

It will be instead an urban place like the one described by a fourth grader:

The housing is like an
apartment full of people
crowded in all together.
We all feel squashed in
when everybody comes home
from work and watches television.

More recently, I have been involved in attempting to prevent further expansion of the Kahului Airport before proper environmental studies are conducted to determine the effects of airport expansion on Maui and its resident populations of plants, animals, insects, and people.

Either we will be successful at preventing the internationalization of Maui's airport or we may find ourselves in the future forced to live a life as dystopian as the one depicted in the movie *Total Recall*. Each of us has an important choice to make.

The two poems featured on page 8 appeared in *Haku Mele O Hawaii*—the first poem in vol. VIII (1981) and the second poem in vol. IX (1982)— published by the Office of Instructional Services, Department of Education, State of Hawaiʻi.

Crossing the Pali

We're all young enough
to remember
what it was like
when we were growing up
in Hilo small town or Kāne'ohe
where it rained rivers of
red dirt in the winter
from all the new-cut hillsides.
There's still the suggestion
of old streams and lo'i
under the sunken lawns.
My grandfather had a house
stepping down to a small
stream hidden like a secret,
the shy green spring
of a young girl flowing
in the shade of a mango tree.
Years later we went
away to college climbing
the peaks of Western thought.
But I remember the stories—
my uncle sleeping on the beach
in a hole lined with newspaper,
his youngest brother not far away
in his own hole for the night.
In the morning they gathered
coconuts that had fallen
from the night sky.

On the other side of the island,
my mother's popo is cooking
bird's nest soup in the kitchen.
One of my father's sisters
had a husband who used to twirl
knives for the Samoan fire dance,
which he perfected and later performed
somewhere on the east coast.
Another sister lived in Maple Shade,
New Jersey, while the rest of us
grew thick as bamboo in Kāneʻohe.
These people are still around
like the brightly colored fish
swimming in the aquarium at
my grand aunt's house in Kaimukī.
I know that you have the same
kinds of stories lined up
the way you used to line up
with your father, mother
and brothers all in a row
at Saint Joseph's on Sundays.
Now you're an attorney
and you act different.
You part your hair
in the middle. You look like
you never get enough sleep.
You're almost always
in an office, 27th floor,
air conditioning, mirrored windows,
in downtown Honolulu,
and you think the guys
riding around with big tires
and tinted glass are funny.
Look at you, you don't go
to the beach, you say

you don't have fun, you work
too hard and for what?
So the big Japanese company
can carve up the coast
like so much raw tuna.
Very refreshing with a little
Kirin after a round of golf.
Meanwhile another company
from Wyoming wants to drill
deep into the mountain directly
above your client's new resort
to extract high-temperature
steam for electricity.
Never mind that the gases
escaping with the steam
will smell like rotten eggs.
Worry about that when the time comes.
It's almost midnight
on the day when you questioned me
for more than six hours
about my interest in keeping
the old road in Mākena open
to traffic of all kinds.
All the while, hammering away
for the developer who wants
everybody off the beach before
the hotel opens in late summer.
It's almost midnight
under the same moon.

Who says you have to go along with it?

Early Mākena Road protest. Former governor George Ariyoshi in the first golf cart, and then-governor John Waihe'e in the second, ferry the prime minister of Japan and a top Seibu executive across the sandy track of Mākena Road. They are met by a small band of protestors including longtime Maui County council member Wayne Nishiki with three of his children, and Dana Naone Hall with a nearly three-year-old Leahi Hall.

Photograph by Masako Cordray.

Public Hearing on Resolution No. 84-139, Concerning the Mākena Road

4

MAUI COUNTY COUNCIL

NOVEMBER 27, 1984

Aloha ahiahi, council members. My name is Dana Naone Hall. I am thankful that the decision about whether to close or keep open the makai Mākena Road is a public one. What we are talking about is finding a way to live with one another. It is not a matter of dominance or ownership and property rights, or the trading of one important and essential use of a place for another. But finding each other on the same island, who will make room for whom, and how will we do it?

Rather than talk of exclusion, how can we make it possible to accommodate two apparently opposed points of view, which have arisen because of the proposed exchange? If the terms of the exchange were altered, the opposition would vanish. The sore point is the road. Many of us here favor the plan for a state park at Mākena, but not at the expense of the road. The state has made a generous number of acres available for selection by Seibu* in exchange for the 8 acres at Oneloa, so the road is not essential for a fair monetary exchange. Yet the value of the road to Native Hawaiians and other longtime users of it cannot be assessed in terms of money. It has no

* Seibu refers to, collectively, Seibu Hawaii Inc., Seibu Fudōsan Kabushiki Kaisha and Prince Hotels of Hawaii Inc.

price, but forms an important link to the Hawaiian culture as it lives in this moment.

I have heard a representative of Seibu declare, "The people destroyed the trail." But the trail has not been destroyed, it has been kept alive by continuous and traditional use for more than 400 years. No one expects anything 400 years old to look the way it did when it first appeared in the world. If we had lives that spanned four centuries, we would not look the same at 10 or 20 as we would look at 100 or 300, or in this case—400. The road has evolved the way we, as a people, have evolved over the course of these many years.

What does trail and road mean anyway? In Hawaiian it is Ke Alaloa—the way to travel from one place to another. This particular way keeps close to the shoreline, and those of us who travel on it today know the refreshment it gives to be only a few steps away from the ocean, wrapped in sea air and the long-looked-for glimpse, through the gray companion kiawe, of white sand where it meets the breaking waves and the splash of warm blue water. The new mauka road would move us 800 to 1,000 feet farther away from the shore. It would move us off our ancestral trail and away from our long tradition of already established access to the beaches, bays, and rocky places of the coast.

This does not have to happen. Let us agree to reach a harmonious decision that upholds the rights and wishes of the people of Maui to come and go along the road, and to mingle freely on the beaches—residents and visitors alike.

It is my deep hope that the council will act to accommodate our interests rather than set them up in competition with Seibu's wishes. If Seibu can understand the importance of the road to the people who live here, and give up its request to close the road, then we will have found a way to all live together.

We are asking in the gentlest and most persistent way we know to please keep the road open.

The Year of the Hawaiian

5

PUBLIC INFORMATIONAL MEETING
SPONSORED BY HUI ALANUI O MĀKENA
AT MAUI COMMUNITY COLLEGE
1987

Thank you all for coming tonight. We began this year with a Sierra Club meeting organized by Hui Alanui o Mākena in February on the topic of "Maui's Coastline: Public or Private?" and I remember well the sense of renewed hope and determination with which we greeted the coming year and the work before us.

I know I felt that one way or another we would have to make the best use of the propitious circumstances offered to us by the Year of the Hawaiian and, in particular, I hoped that it would be possible to break through on the Mākena Road issue and make substantial gains for Native Hawaiian and public rights.

As many of you are aware, the Hui did negotiate a Settlement Agreement with Seibu Hawaii in July, the result of three years of unrelenting pressure and six lawsuits. To simplify things greatly, perhaps our best tactic was that we would not go away. In fact, we were constantly in the way on every procedural occasion. The Hui challenged Seibu at every Maui County Council meeting, including committee meetings, and on every occasion before the Maui County Planning Commission. As Isaac said earlier, it was the environmental claims raised in the various lawsuits that advanced us furthest on the legal front.

The Hui is concerned about the entire length of the existing

Mākena Road, and following the Settlement Agreement in July, the county council passed a resolution that directs corporation counsel to continue with the condemnation of another section of Mākena Road, at Palauea, with the added stipulation that the purpose of the condemnation action is "for public road purposes."

So there have been victories to celebrate and be thankful for since the beginning of the year.

One of the things that kept us going was the feeling that there is an immense amount of support in the community for what the Hui is doing. I don't mean to say that the support is for the Hui's efforts alone, but for the Hui's part in making sure that decisions involving the use of our lands and ocean are not adverse to the public's interests. A great many people care about what is happening to Maui.

We are not celebrating any particular anniversary in the Year of the Hawaiian, as was the case with the Kanyaku Imin celebrations commemorating the hundredth anniversary of the arrival of Japanese people to Hawai'i. Instead, we are celebrating our survival as a culturally distinct people in the place of our birth.

Coastal Zone Management Area Hearing, Ocean Resources and Beach Access

6

LAHAINA CIVIC CENTER

SEPTEMBER 30, 1987

We have a problem on Maui where a number of beaches that have always been accessible have been closed off in the last ten years or so, and the present county administration's position has been to tie the regaining of beach access to development, generally hotel development, of the shoreline. Of course, by the time the hotel or condominiums go in, any access that is opened up for the public is of a secondary nature to that enjoyed by the hotels and their guests. Purposefully so, I might add.

It's easy to support this opinion. After all, there are very few visitors to our islands who have or would be likely to complain about inadequate access to sandy beaches—particularly those in front of the hotels that they may be staying at. The development of our shoreline areas has been tailored to the needs of these guests to our shores. It's the person who lives here, and doesn't have a perch in a $100- or $200-dollar-a-day room, who has a gripe about access.

The coastal zones of our islands have proven to be very vulnerable to lax administration on the county level of the Special Management Area (SMA) permit process. Our coastal resources are not being protected as is mandated by the Coastal Zone Management Act, and the ability of the entire cross section of our resident society to fully use the coastal zone area has become increasingly restricted.

At the same time, the proliferation of uses by the tourist industry is on the increase.

One example: six months ago, Makena Boat Partners requested mooring permits for a catamaran operation in Mākena. The catamarans had been moored illegally for some months, and numerous complaints were made before the company was moved to seek mooring permits.

At the Board of Land and Natural Resources meeting on Maui at which the board received testimony on the mooring permit application, several residents testified against granting the permit, citing numerous violations, including the dumping of trash from the catamaran into the water and bringing the catamaran within a few feet of the shoreline to allow passengers to disembark. I witnessed one such occasion where the catamaran hove into the shallow water with the boat's crew waving swimmers out of the way.

I believe that the board issued the mooring permit, and the public is once again put in the position of having to keep an eye out for violations, which, even if reported, rarely elicit quick, if any, action. If an operation is conducting business illegally, I think it makes more sense to close it down for a time before considering the granting of any necessary permits. Otherwise, it's business as usual and a commercial venture that was in violation before receiving a permit is unlikely to discontinue its easygoing ways afterward.

I have one more comment: the legislature passed a law that allows the planning commissions of our different counties to reclassify land that is 15 acres or less in size. This means owners of parcels of land that meet the size restriction don't need to apply to the State Land Use Commission for reclassification, but can seek reclassification on the county level. The reason I raise this land use issue is because I'm concerned that owners of parcels larger than 15 acres, who intend to develop the entire acreage, will subdivide their parcel so that it is possible to slip under the 15-acre limit, as separate but contiguous parcels, and reclassify agricultural lands to urban before a less rigorous reviewing body. I'm concerned about this because a district boundary amendment and land use reclassification is being sought for agricultural lands in Wailea, which, if approved, would create more urban land out of one of the last remaining pieces of land of any size makai of Wailea Alanui Road in the Wailea area.

The relation to beach access is this: in the past two months the Maui Planning Commission approved SMA permits for the Four Seasons Hotel, a 400-room luxury hotel makai of the road at Wailea, followed closely by approval for the proposed Wailea Grand Hyatt—an 800-room luxury hotel next door to the Four Seasons—and coming up, the reclassification from agriculture to urban of an approximately 14.91-acre parcel adjoining these proposed hotels, which will allow Embassy Suites Hotel to seek an SMA for a hotel with several hundred suites.

The density of development planned for Wailea assures a virtual lockout of the larger resident community to near shore and shoreline lands, and the ocean. The situation is bad enough now, it is already a degradation of local residents' use of the area prior to the the early 1970s when the first hotels in the Wailea Resort were built.

Development is not such a benign creature after all. The coral from Kīhei to Mākena is in bad shape. The coral past Mākena Landing and moving south along the coast toward Keoneʻōʻio is still alive, likely because the line of development has not extended much past that point—yet. This is a symbol of the poʻe, the people of Hawaiʻi, who, like the coral, thrive when they are not overrun.

Wailea Beach Villas Project, Special Management Area Permit

7

MAUI PLANNING COMMISSION HEARING

JULY 10, 2001

Good afternoon, commissioners. My name is Dana Naone Hall. I am here today to again request that if the commission decides to approve a Special Management Area (SMA) permit for the Wailea Beach Villas, that it add a condition to the permit approval requiring that mauka–makai public access from Wailea Alanui to the shoreline within the project area be provided along with dedicated on-site public parking for beach access purposes.

Lateral shoreline access is not the issue; adequate lateral access exists. However, mauka–makai access to the lateral shoreline walkway within the Wailea Resort is inadequate for members of the public who do not happen to be guests at one of the hotels or condominiums makai of Wailea Alanui.

Page 45 of the Environmental Assessment (EA) for this project recites sections of chapter 205a-26 of the Hawaii Coastal Zone Management Act. Subsection (1) states:

> All development in the special management area *shall* be subject to reasonable terms and conditions set by the authority in order to ensure: (A) Adequate access, by dedication or other means, to publicly owned or used beaches, recreation areas, and natural reserves is provided to the extent consistent with sound conservation principles. (Emphasis added)

According to the EA, the coastal portion of the property consists of approximately 440 feet of shoreline frontage. The majority of the shoreline is along a rocky point, but more than 100 feet, and perhaps as much as 150 feet, is along a sandy beach. I would ask the commissioners to look at various figures in the EA, including figure 3A.

This project has been designed, like so many other projects in Mākena–Wailea, as an exclusive enclave—high-end housing far beyond the reach of the majority of Maui's residents.

Because the property is in an undeveloped state at the moment, I have seen people park in the Shops at Wailea parking lot and walk down to the north end of Wailea Beach Villas property. The nearest mauka–makai public beach accesses currently in existence are the Ulua/Mōkapu beach access located 0.5 miles to the north of the project area and the Wailea Beach access located 0.4 miles to the south, as indicated in the EA.

The lateral shoreline walkway is nearly a mile long between the mauka–makai accesses at Ulua/Mōkapu Beach and Wailea Beach. The provision of a mauka–makai access within the Wailea Beach Villas development would greatly enhance the public's ability to use and enjoy Wailea Beach. The current Wailea Beach public access is at the southern end of the beach. Wailea Beach is close to 1,300 feet in length.

I don't understand how it can be a burden on the developer to provide mauka–makai access and 6 to 12 parking stalls for public beach access when the project itself involves the construction of eight residential buildings including a five-story penthouse building containing 64 units, as well as 204 parking stalls for project residents. Adding 6 to 12 parking stalls for the public is an extremely modest addition. The public interest and the Coastal Zone Management Act would be served by providing mauka–makai access and on-site parking for the public.

Government Beach Reserve Lands, Conservation District Use Application Permit Violations

8

BOARD OF LAND AND NATURAL RESOURCES

JULY 8, 1994

Good morning, Chairperson Keith Ahue and board members. I'm here today on behalf of Hui Alanui o Mākena and Keauhou o Honua'ula. Both the Hui and Keauhou support the actions taken by your staff to require the immediate correction of certain important discrepancies by the applicant, and the recommendation that this board find the applicant in violation of conditions 20 and 21 of the Conservation District Use Application (CDUA) permit.

Recent events support staff's initial detailed report and recommendation for denial of the CDUA permit request. I bring to your attention again the reasons given by the applicant's son, Don Carlsberg, for seeking the CDUA permit to landscape state beach reserve lands. According to the minutes of your February 11, 1994, meeting, he said that "his view was obstructed and that the landscaping would help resolve the problem of dust and dirt blowing around." Staff analysis aptly noted that this hardship was self-imposed when the parcel was illegally filled and graded without appropriate authorization.

Mr. Carlsberg also indicated that "it would enable him to use his patio without worrying about dirt." Perhaps we should commend Mr. Carlsberg for his honest statement of the private benefits he sought to secure by obtaining a landscaping easement for important public shoreline land. The wonder is that the board agreed to cloak the undeniable and primarily private aspects of this request in the robe of benefits that would be conferred on the public.

Adequate public and traditional access to this land existed until relatively recent times when new landowners like the applicant took actions to secure the maximum use and benefit of their private property, at times at the expense of the public's and Native Hawaiian traditional and customary use of adjacent lands. Once the private use is established, any encroachments on and/or private use of public lands are justified by the alleged benefits to the public.

These are the same kinds of self-serving circular arguments used by hotel developers on this island. It is our belief that general public and, in particular, Native Hawaiian access to and use of shoreline lands in Maui's primary resort areas of Kāʻanapali and Wailea, for example, have diminished since the development of these resorts. The de facto privatization of other publicly owned coastal areas and beaches by private entities only exacerbates the problem.

Please remember that the effective closing off of the beaches and shoreline to the general public, and the curtailment or constriction of traditional and customary access, is a historically recent situation. It is a situation that should not be and does not have to be perpetuated.

Today the board has the opportunity to require the restoration of this shoreline land illegally filled by the permit holder and in the process restore some measure of public trust in the board. Therefore, we support the public interests that would be served in revocation of the CDUA permit.

Palauea Preserve

9

EXCERPTED FROM *KA WAI OLA O OHA*
JULY 2014

The June 17, 2014, ceremony to mark the return of our lāhui's stewardship to the 20-acre Palauea cultural preserve was preceded by a sign from the heavens. On a bright, sunny late afternoon on Maui's south coast, a dark line of clouds, extending from the upper slope of Haleakalā toward Kaho'olawe, suddenly appeared. Rain fell from the nāulu cloud formation, accompanied by a strong breeze that ruffled the surface of the ocean.

The sky cleared when several dozen individuals assembled for a ceremonial blessing led by University of Hawai'i Maui College Hawaiian Studies and Hawaiian Language professors.

During the blessing, Hui Alanui o Mākena's early efforts to reconnect to the coastal land at Palauea by reopening access to the sandy shoreline, and by preventing attempts by developers to close the Palauea portion of the Mākena–Keone'ō'io Road, were recounted. (This road is shown on mid-nineteenth-century maps as the aupuni or government road, whose location is believed to be in the approximate alignment of the Pi'ilani Trail established in the sixteenth century.)

Efforts to protect Palauea began in the 1980s and intensified in the following decades to include the preservation of archaeological and cultural sites. Archaeological evidence indicated long-term habitation of the area, and the 20-acre preserve includes ceremonial places and site complexes, numerous habitation sites, and hundreds of agricultural and other features. Years of lobbying government officials in Maui County and a sympathetic landowner-developer resulted in the recognition that this land required protection.

With Palauea poised for preservation, Maui developer Everett Dowling transferred the land to the Office of Hawaiian Affairs. Now physical stewardship of the land is in the capable hands of the University of Hawaiʻi Maui College Hawaiian Studies Department under whose guidance high school and college students practice malama ʻāina at Palauea.

There is precedent for Palauea. Twenty years ago, in May 1994, at a ceremony on Palauea's shore, a deed returning Kahoʻolawe to Hawaiʻi was signed by the US Navy, Governor John Waiheʻe, and a member of the Protect Kahoʻolawe ʻOhana. Hoʻokupu was taken in canoes to the ocean and hoʻokupu was also offered at a heiau in the future preserve.

The message from those conducting the recent June ceremony was one of reaffirming our connection to the land where new moʻolelo about our lāhui will arise. In caring for the land, we will learn from the land, and together we will grow and flourish.

Palauea is a place where the sun is strong and a sovereign wind blows.

Excerpt adapted from "Native Stewardship of Palauea," *Ka Wai Ola o OHA* 31, no. 7 (July 2014): 5.

The nāulu cloud formation releases life-giving rain on the northern end of Kahoʻolawe.
Photograph by Isaac Hall and Dana Naone Hall.

Going to Kaho'olawe

By boat the island appeared
pale and purple under a milky sky.
Whale known blue ocean
quilted with waves,
we swim ashore in the morning rain.
Olivine crystals jewel the beach.
We are not the first.
Dusty-backed scorpions in the garden,
rats and feral cats stare
out of their night
at what we have brought with us.
Goats keep out of the way
up the red ravines.
Wasps multiply in the bamboo poles
of the cook house.
Standing inside the wall of the heiau
one of the men talks
about the life of the stones.
He holds one up for us to see
black black stone pōhaku
        the mixing of the waters
        the planting of the fields
I am squatting in my own right of way,
he says, and night comes on.
We sleep in the sound of the creaking trees.
A low yellow light wakes me
far from the traffic of the island
we have come from where
the headlights of an orange truck
look out to sea.

Kahoʻolawe Conveyance Commission Meeting 11

MAY 14, 1991

For many of us, Hawaiians in particular, Kahoʻolawe has been a turning point. What direction are we headed in now? That is something that this commission will help to determine: whether Kahoʻolawe, and all of us, experience a new beginning—or whether the military is allowed to continue to have limited use of the island in the future.

I hope that this commission will include among its recommendations a complete cessation of military use, and that the immediate return of the island to the transitional jurisdiction of the state of Hawaiʻi (prior to its ultimate conveyance to a sovereign Native Hawaiian entity) be conditioned by a clear ban on any commercial activities on the island and in the near shore waters.

The threat posed by the military's use of Kahoʻolawe can be easily replaced by the no less destructive threat posed by the operation of commercial activities on the island.

I learned today of a South Shore Adventure being promoted by a commercial rafting operation operating out of the Kīhei Boat Ramp. This operation charges $75 to take snorkelers and curiosity seekers beyond La Pérouse, or Keoneʻōʻio Bay, along the coast of the ʻĀhihi-Kīnaʻu Natural Area Reserve to "snorkel over coral pinnacles and swim with the turtles in pristine waters."

It will be very difficult to control the operation of commercial tour boat operators, as only one example of the problems that will occur, if it is not made clear from the very beginning that commercial operations will be banned from the island.

The illegal landings of the future may not be the Protect Kahoʻolawe ʻOhana claiming its own, but the surreptitious landing of zodiacs bringing snorkelers and picnickers in for a closer look.

Letter to Noa Emmett Aluli and the Kahoʻolawe Island Reserve Commission Regarding the Hawaii Island Shallow Water Training Range Proposed for Interisland Channel Waters between Maui, Lānaʻi, and Kahoʻolawe

12

MAY 12, 1999

The US Navy is planning to establish and install the Hawaii Island Shallow Water Training Range (HISWTR) within a sixty square nautical mile area in the interisland channel waters between Maui, Lānaʻi, and Kahoʻolawe. The Naval Undersea Warfare Center and the Pacific Missile Range Facility (PMRF) on Kauaʻi are involved in seeking approvals for and implementing HISWTR.

The Naval Undersea Warfare Center has initiated Section 106 consultation pursuant to the National Historic Preservation Act for the HISWTR project. We have urged the US Navy project engineers to include the Kahoʻolawe Island Reserve Commission (Commission) as a consulting party. We believe that the Commission should engage in consultation with the navy and PMRF pursuant to the National Historic Preservation Act *and* the National Environmental Policy Act, and conduct a thorough review of the proposed project for the following reasons:

- It is not clear that the proposed project, and the military activities it is designed to monitor and facilitate, will not encroach upon or affect the restricted waters surrounding the island of Kahoʻolawe. The proposed project is an expansion of an existing Hawaiian Area Underwater Tracking System (HATS) used for submarine training exercises, including the firing of inert torpedoes. The Final Environmental Assessment for the HATS project, prepared in June 1994 for the Naval Undersea Warfare Center Detachment, includes figure 7, which shows a submerged submarine operating area located, in part, within the restricted waters that are subject to the Commission's jurisdiction.

- Hawai'i Revised Statutes Section 6K-3(a) states that the Kaho'olawe Island Reserve shall be used solely and exclusively for four enumerated purposes, none of which include military activities.
- Even if the navy represents that none of its military activities will take place within the Reserve, the boundaries of the Reserve are not marked in the water, either on the surface or beneath the surface, and it would be nearly impossible to monitor the underwater activities of the navy and conduct effective enforcement operations.
- The Commission is charged with the responsibility for assuring that the Reserve will only be used for permitted purposes. The Commission is also responsible for providing advice to government officials and agencies on any matter relating to the Reserve.
- The navy's use of immediately adjacent waters for military purposes can have significant adverse impacts on the Reserve and resources protected within the Reserve.
- Many past and present members of the Protect Kaho'olawe 'Ohana, as well as numerous other individuals and organizations, worked diligently to demilitarize Kaho'olawe and certainly would not accept the remilitarization or continued militarization of an adjoining area.

A letter dated April 15, 1999, which details some of the concerns that we have already expressed directly to the navy about its project, was sent earlier to the Commission. We will not reiterate all of the points made in that letter but hope you will review its contents.

We believe this is an important matter that should be considered as soon as possible by the Commission. We would urge that you place this matter on the agenda of the Commission's next regularly scheduled meeting, which we understand is set for June 4, 1999. We further request that this meeting be held on the island of Maui so that Hui Alanui o Mākena, Keauhou o Honuaʻula and other interested members of the Native Hawaiian community and public will have the opportunity to address the Commission on these significant issues.

Sunlight on the fan-shaped leaves of a loulu palm (a native Pritchardia*). There are twenty-three Pritchardia species that are native to the Islands, most of which are in danger of extinction in their natural habitats.*
Photograph by Elizabeth Carton.

Native Species

13

One day we went to see Rene,
who is descended from Hawaiians on both sides—
though he bears the French name of a family friend—
and found him at work in the botanical
garden that is full of Hawaiian plants
started from seedlings he grew himself.
We passed the fat black goats in their pen
unlike the ones on Kahoʻolawe
that the Navy has promised to get rid of
or to keep the population so low
they won't get into the new plants
Rene plans to take to the island
after the first rains of the Makahiki
have settled the dust. Two thousand
to begin with, *all native species*.
When those cover the ground
in thick profusion and the scent
of hinahina is in the air again,
the shrubs will be planted.
Once they're established in native ground
places will be prepared for the trees.
All of this he tells us with his hands
clasped and resting lightly on his stomach
as we stand in the shade of the kukui tree.
Native species listening to talk about native species.
The native plants are disappearing, he says,
they're loosing their habitat
and they're prey to ignorance and laziness
as much as to greed.

Out comes the story of the two Hawaiian coconuts
old trees that lived next to a brackish well
along the dry coast at Mākena, near the bay
where the ʻōʻio were once as thick as sand.
Not long ago, someone came along and wanted
the nuts from one of the trees and cut it down.
The other tree is still there
but there won't be any more seedlings.
The male flower always blooms first
and after it dies the female flower blooms.
A single tree cannot make love to itself
and without another nearby of its species
there will be no more young trees.
Then there's the hao, named for Maui,
that he found growing along the same coast.
One of the trees is so old he suspects
it was there when La Pérouse came into the bay—
in the company of his own kind,
among the first white men to lay eyes on Maui.
Sometimes on his walks he comes across
a plant growing in isolation. When that happens
he says he asks himself why is the noni here?

I start thinking I'm living 300 years ago
I get one malo on.
I'm thinking what I'm doing here
what kind grass is over here I need
for my house down the beach
or my canoe or for my fishing net.
Sometimes I get crazy walking
On the lava thinking about the plants.

By now we're following him around, hot and crazy
in the sun ourselves, walking on the lava,
and then he says *The Hawaiian plants are social plants.*

If you go look underneath the Hawaiian tree
There's all kinds of plants that grow under them.
Ferns and vines and shrubs and other kinds of trees.
They all grow together under the Hawaiian tree.
But the nonnative plants are antisocial trees
like kiawe or the eucalyptus or the ironwood.
Go down to the beach sometime he tells us
and look at the ironwood tree, the mature
ironwood tree, nothing grows under there.
They don't like anybody else except
for one species, their own kind.
We figure we know what he's talking about
and we laugh.
I also figure that these plants are still
in the world because Rene knows their names.
He knows where they come from
and how to keep them straight
kolomona, nehe, ʻāwikiwiki, naio.
That's because he knows where he comes from
and he doesn't tell us but we understand
it's up to us to trace
our genealogy through the native species
and to get to know our own kinds.

Testimony on Native Hawaiian Education Act 14

KAHULUI

MARCH 20, 1994

Aloha, congress members. Welcome home. We would like to begin by extending our mahalo for your support, over the years, of federal funding for Native Hawaiian educational opportunities, and for your current efforts on behalf of the Native Hawaiian Education Act. Coming from Maui , we also want to acknowledge Representative Patsy Mink's vigorous advocacy of the Native Hawaiian Education Act earlier this month, which was instrumental in defeating an amendment that would have eliminated the Act altogether.

In support of the Native Hawaiian Education Act, we offer the following statements and suggested revisions.

The Pūnana Leo program began on Maui in 1987 with twelve students. The preschool is presently operating at maximum capacity with twenty-six students. Interest in the program has grown tremendously in the nearly seven years since the first preschoolers on Maui were greeted in Hawai'i's mother language. This year, we already have fifty children and their parents waiting to be interviewed for the sixteen openings that will be available this September. The strong interest in the Pūnana Leo program, particularly in the Native Hawaiian community, delights us and also challenges us all to meet the growing needs of our community.

The present facility in Central Maui can accommodate no more than twenty-six students; however, if a larger facility were available, enrollment would easily double. In addition, parents of preschoolers in distant Lahaina and Hāna would like to see Pūnana Leo sites established in their districts.

One primary reason for this island-wide (and statewide) interest is that the Pūnana Leo program requires the active participation of the preschoolers' families. Parents and/or guardians of children enrolled in the program are committed to working a minimum of eight hours a month for the school, in addition to attending a weekly Hawaiian language class and meeting as a parents' group once a month.

These commitments provide a supportive context for our young students and, as importantly, directly engage families in the educational process. Pūnana Leo has always been family based and, by its nature, the program reinforces important Hawaiian cultural values by encouraging the continued practice of these values within not only the immediate family but also the larger cultural group.

There are many instances in which the enrollment of one child has resulted in not only parents but grandparents, uncles, aunts, siblings, and even friends of the family becoming involved in the program through its language- and culture-based activities. While the actual numbers of Pūnana Leo graduates may appear to be relatively small, these children are really at the center of a much larger support group—all of whom share in the educational and cultural benefits.

For these reasons, we support the inclusion of the Pūnana Leo project in Section 2805, "Native Hawaiian Language Immersion Authority." Because Section 2805 relates specifically and solely to "revitalizing the Native Hawaiian language," we feel that it would also be appropriate to include a specific reference to ʻAha Pūnana Leo in Section 2806, "Native Hawaiian Family-Based Education Centers." The ʻAha Pūnana Leo activities are very much consistent with the described purposes of family-based education centers contained in Section 3806 (a)(1)-(4).

Mahalo.

Building a Parking Lot in the Wailuku Historic District

MAUI COUNTY CULTURAL RESOURCES COMMISSION MEETING
FEBRUARY 4, 2016

There is no final Environmental Assessment (EA) for the County of Maui Employee 67-Stall Parking Lot, and the draft EA submitted to the Office of Environmental Quality Control in March 2012 is nearly four years old, outdated and, in any event, inadequate. Even so, the draft EA acknowledges in the preface on page 1 and, again, on page 5 that the project site is located within Wailuku Historic District 3 and historic district approval is required.

As stated by Annalise Kehler, county cultural resource planner, in the June 4, 2015, meeting minutes of the Cultural Resources Commission (CRC): "The CRC has the authority to approve all plans in the county historic districts." This authority is explicit in chapter 19.52.020 of the Maui County Code titled "Review of Plans."

Four historic buildings occupy the western or mauka half of a 2.65-acre parcel of land owned by Wailuku Union Church. The county parking lot project is proposed for the eastern or makai half of the parcel. It should be noted that the proposed project area is approximately 30,000 square feet in size—well over a half acre. The parking lot will extend from Aupuni Street to Main Street, causing significant visual impacts in the heart of Historic District 3.

In addition, significant effects on air quality due to emissions from vehicles, as well as noise impacts from vehicles, especially during

Incoming! Maui's Multimillion-Dollar Airport Expansion Doesn't Make Sense

16

HONOLULU WEEKLY

JANUARY 1, 1992

As a fifteen-year resident of the island of Maui, I often find myself casting a wary eye across the Pailolo and Kaiwi Channels in the direction of the island where I was born and raised, O'ahu. For many of us concerned about the rising costs of the economic development of the Hawaiian Islands, the view is grim.

While residents of O'ahu wrestle with the issue of a multibillion-dollar mass transit system, another enormous expansion of the transportation system is going virtually unnoticed—or at least unchallenged. At a price of just under $2 billion, the Hawai'i Department of Transportation (DOT) is currently expanding Honolulu's International Airport to accommodate a passenger increase of 72 percent from 1989 to the year 2010.

There have been well-publicized pronouncements from the visitor industry, most notably from Hawaii Visitors Bureau president Stanley Hong, about "intolerable" delays in processing foreign visitors through Immigration and Customs at Honolulu International—particularly during peak morning periods when flights, primarily from Japan, arrive in rapid succession. These pronouncements require a context: Honolulu International, currently the ninth busiest airport in the United States, ranks fourth in the nation in the number of international arrivals (behind New York's John F. Kennedy International Airport, Miami International, and Los Angeles International). This immense amount of air traffic is occurring in an island state that contains less than 1 percent of the country's total land area.

The airport hit a high of more than 23 million passengers in 1990; if projections remain on course, the year 2010 should bring nearly 37 million passengers. The biggest jump in numbers is projected to occur among Mainland and international passengers—with the numbers expected to more than double from 12.8 million in 1989 to 26 million in 2010. Again, a context may prove helpful. Los Angeles International Airport played host to 45 million passengers in 1990, while at San Francisco, the nation's next-busiest airport, 31 million passengers arrived and departed.

The overwhelming increase of visitors expected to travel to the state in the next decade also puts pressure on the Neighbor Islands. At the moment, Maui is waging a tough battle with the DOT over the department's expansion plans for Kahului Airport. The expansion is designed to accommodate some of the "leaking" that airports administrator Owen Miyamoto expects from Honolulu. It is also designed to encourage more direct overseas flights to Neighbor Island destinations. The Maui County Council voted recently to include in an update of the county's general plan strong language against turning Kahului Airport into an international facility and opposing the extension of the airport's 7,000-foot runway. The current runway length imposes weight restrictions on wide-bodied jet aircraft operating between Maui and the West Coast. Several citizens' groups and Maui County Council members have taken the position that any extension of the runway is likely to make Kahului Airport more attractive and, therefore, more vulnerable to domestic and foreign airlines seeking new routes—particularly from Japan to Maui.

Maui's ability to gain some control over the rapid rate of development that has taken place on the island in the last decade (which ushered in, among other things, the largest increase in resident population in the state—42 percent on Maui versus the state average of 17 percent) lies in its ability to control the number of visitors pouring into the island. Much of the growth of recent years, for good and ill, has been generated by the visitor industry. Construction has been a major contributor too, much of it connected to the building of hotels and other visitor accommodation facilities.

Although O'ahu welcomes by far the largest number of tourists, the visitors are more readily absorbed given the island's population base. On any given day on O'ahu, one out of every 10 people is a visitor. On the Valley Isle, 3 to 4 of every 10 people are visitors. The perception that Maui is feeling the effects of a burgeoning tourism industry more sharply than anywhere else in the state is well founded. Maui's roads, sewers, and available water are taxed to the limit. Maui's schools, its only hospital, and the rest of its social services are in need of additional funding and expansion. The planned expansion of Kahului Airport will cost an estimated $189 million. In its current state, the airport can already accommodate a 91 percent increase in passengers; pouring millions more into the facility doesn't make sense.

Calls for growth management on Maui are hardly an indication of the not-in-my-backyard syndrome. Maui has a solid 25 percent of the entire number of transient accommodation units (hotel rooms, condominiums, and so on) in the state. Maui's transient accommodations inventory represents approximately 52 percent of the Neighbor Islands' total, and the number of Maui's transient accommodation units and its visitor count is roughly equal to the combined count for the Big Island and Kauai. Maui's backyard and its beaches are already full.

If the expected vast increases in visitors spill over to the Neighbor Islands, so too will the big-city problems of Honolulu: homelessness, lack of affordable housing, massive sewage spills, increasing urbanization, and the continuing degradation of Hawai'i's unique environment. Our citizenry must be informed, and then we must tell our government and industry decision-makers that enough is enough. Then, amid the distractions of modern life, we can pause to consider again the rainy summit of Wai'ale'ale, the green heights of Ka'ala, the radiance of Haleakalā, and the snow and fiery reaches of Mauna Kea and Mauna Loa. This is a Hawai'i worth protecting for future generations.

Kanahā Pond State Wildlife Sanctuary, adjacent to Kahului Airport, is home to the endangered long-legged Hawaiian stilt or ae'o (shown), as well as the 'alae ke'oke'o, Hawaiian coot, and the koloa maoli, Hawaiian duck.
Photograph by Masako Cordray.

Longer Doesn't Mean Safer 17

LETTER TO THE EDITOR OF THE *MAUI NEWS*

MAY 29, 1992

Maui Chamber of Commerce President Wayne Hedani's letter (May 13, 1992) attacking an earlier letter by Lyle Bettger (April 28, 1992) on the Kahului Airport runway issue deserves a response.

To shore up his side, Mr. Hedani refers to the often-invoked testimony of the Air Line Pilots Association (ALPA). Mr. Hedani fails to note the caveat contained in ALPA's comments: "While we do not consider the Maui Airport unsafe, there are many improvements that could enhance the airport's margin of safety." ALPA proposed several "safety enhancements," which invite no argument and should be implemented; however, the recommendation that Runway 2-20 be extended may create, rather than solve, safety problems.

ALPA does not address the issue of providing adequate runway safety areas on both ends of Runway 2-20. Runway safety areas are designed for the rare emergency situations when an aircraft may overrun or undershoot a runway. A longer runway will not result in an increase in the length of the runway safety areas.

Extension to 8,500, 9,500, or 10,500 feet would be capped by the same 1,000-foot runway safety areas. While a longer runway would make it possible for larger and heavier aircraft (for example, 747s) to land and take off, the margin of safety at Kahului would remain essentially unchanged. The construction of 2,000-foot-long runway safety areas on both ends of Runway 2-20 would provide the additional safety desired by anyone concerned with existing conditions at Kahului Airport.

At its current length, Runway 2-20 fits neatly into the area bounded by Hāna Highway and the Spreckelsville coastline with room available to increase the runway safety areas. Lengthening the active runway will diminish the buffer between the runway and Hāna Highway. For instance, the mauka end of a 1,000-foot runway safety area serving a 9,500-foot runway would have to be built within several hundred feet of Hāna Highway. It would appear that aircraft approaching an extended Runway 2-20 would have to fly in at lower elevations over Hāna Highway in order to touch down 1,500 to 2,500 feet closer to the highway than is presently the case. On the makai end, a runway extension to 10,500 feet would place a 1,000-foot-long runway safety area virtually on the shoreline, thereby increasing the likelihood that a large plane could end up in the ocean.

The safest runway length given the circumstances at Kahului Airport may be what we already have—a 7,000-foot runway with the addition of longer runway safety areas. In this way the buffers between Hāna Highway and the coastline can be maintained. These buffers are crucial to the overall safety of the airport and surrounding areas.

Instead of scaring the public with not altogether truthful information about airport safety, Mr. Hedani might do better to join in advocating for longer runway safety areas. Otherwise, some of the liability, which he is anxious to assign to council members who voted to include strict language in the General Plan limiting runway lengths, may end up at his doorstep.

Every Day Is Earth Day

18

STATE LAND USE COMMISSION HEARING
APRIL 22, 1999

Aloha, Chairperson Jarman, commissioners and staff. My name is Dana Naone Hall. Thank you for taking time out of your busy lives to come to Maui on Earth Day to hear an issue that has been a source of public debate for 13 years without resolution.

While I sincerely thank you for coming, I am also sorry that you have to be here, and that all of us—whether for or against the Hawaiʻi Department of Transportation's (DOT's) plan—have to be here in the context of a contested proceeding simply because there has never been a good-faith effort by DOT, or any other government official or agency, to bring the various concerned parties together to try to resolve the Kahului Airport issue.

DOT's proposed expansion project, which the pending reclassification request is designed to initiate and facilitate, involves more than 30 individual projects—a number of which are significant, major projects on their own. It is no wonder that this massive multi-component project has fueled more than a decade of controversy.

Complicating matters is an Environmental Impact Statement (EIS) that claims, in its summary volume, that there will be almost no significant adverse impacts caused by the proposed project, particularly for Phases I and II. It is difficult to comprehend how the largest urban-scale project in the history of Maui, costing in excess of $300 million (enough to pay for additional teachers and renovate all 23 of Maui's schools at $13 million per school) will *not* have any

The famous ʻāhinahina (silversword) of Haleakalā, a threatened species, is pollinated by the endangered Hawaiian yellow-faced bee.

Photograph by Kari Robinson.

negative effect on the environment and those of us who live here, especially when projects on a much smaller scale, located in less sensitive areas, and costing far less, are routinely recognized to have significant adverse impacts.

The truth is that the only "no effect" or "no impact" that I know of has been the wider public's ability to influence DOT's airport plan in any significant way. Instead of continuing to play out this matter as Irresistible Force (members of the public) meets Immovable Object (DOT), wouldn't it make more sense and be more productive to direct the parties to negotiate a resolution and settlement of the airport issue?

Enough time, money, and effort has been expended on a conflict that has only served to divide the community. There are countless ways to create divisions among ourselves (newcomers versus long-time residents, environmentalists versus the chamber of commerce), but is this the way we should behave as a society?

For example, the EIS states that approximately 45 percent of Maui's people hold tourism or tourism-related jobs. Indeed, many of us have family and friends who work in the industry, but to presume, as some tourism officials would have us do, that all those working in tourism are de facto supporters of DOT's unmodified airport plan would be a mistake. The views of tourism workers are as diverse as the people in this room. With the perils that led to the violence of Kosovo and Colorado freshly before us, surely there must be a way to honor our differences as we work toward a common understanding and consensus.

Our primary fear is that this hearing, like so many in the past, may be treated as a passing reference to public participation on the way to a predetermined decision. The decision that you make as a commission will profoundly affect our lives and the lives of our children but, more importantly, the life of the place we call Maui. We appeal to you as Maui residents who continue to hope that there may yet be a way to do what is right, so that when you return to your city and towns across the channels that both separate and connect us—the life of this land will continue to be perpetuated for future generations.

State Land Use Commission Meeting, Conclusion of Contested Case Hearing 19

KAHULUI AIRPORT EXPANSION

TESTIMONY OF DANA NAONE HALL

MARCH 23, 2000

Good morning, commissioners. After nearly a year of contested case proceedings, I will be very brief. Although these proceedings have been difficult for everyone involved—none more so than the intervenors—they have resulted in an appropriately just outcome. I do not believe that the governor would have cancelled the Kahului Airport runway extension project if this contested case had not been held and the commission had not been willing to allow in-depth examination and questioning of the many complex issues associated with the Hawai'i Department of Transportation's (DOT's) proposal. This issue (the Kahului Airport expansion) alone argues against the elimination of the State Land Use Commission.

One of our primary concerns has been proper and adequate mitigation of the adverse effects of the proposed airport development—not after-the-fact mitigation, but the implementation of mitigation measures prior to the onset of the adverse impacts. After 14 years and two inadequate Environmental Impact Statement documents, it is time to do things differently. DOT should establish a citizens' advisory committee whose members represent the broad range of interests in our community. This group could function along the lines of similar citizens groups appointed to advise the County of Maui Department of Public Works and the State Highways Division on the Maui Long-Range Land Transportation Plan and the Statewide Long-Range Land Transportation Plan, respectively.

DOT has withdrawn its petition for the moment, but it is not off the hook. Implementation of the Alien Species Action Plan must continue, since the plan is designed to address existing alien species problems as well as future problems that will occur through airport expansion. Furthermore, with or without the runway extension, an analysis of international flight operations must be conducted prior to their initiation.

In closing, I would like to thank the commissioners for your patience and service. Thanks as well to Esther Ueda and Terry Hee, and the rest of the staff, for their courteous and competent help. And, finally, thanks to the hundreds of Maui citizens who participated in these important proceedings. I trust that you will not take offense when I say that I hope not to see the commission again soon —certainly not on this issue.

Mahalo.

Hawaiian Politics Seminar

20

MAUI COMMUNITY COLLEGE

APRIL 20, 2000

The mid-nineteenth century, which centered on the heart of the reign of Kamehameha III, Kauikeaouli, is an appropriate place for me to begin a brief discussion of political issues. During this time, Hawai'i was a part of global trade patterns, and of political maneuvering for power and influence in the Pacific.

In response to foreign pressures, Kauikeaouli, the high chiefs, and missionary advisors, according to Sally Engle Merry in *Colonizing Hawaii: The Cultural Power of Law*, "engaged in transforming the Hawaiian system of law and governance into an Anglo-American political system under the rule of law" (Merry 2000, 4). Their purpose was to create a "civilized nation" that European nations and the United States would recognize as fitting their own notions of sovereignty, thereby preserving, they hoped, the independence of the kingdom.

Three critical changes occurred during Kauikeaouli's time: the establishment of a constitutional monarchy, the institution of private property ownership through the Māhele, and passage of the Kuleana Act of 1850, which in turn led to the rapid expansion of sugar plantations. Before the end of the century, sugar would be king.

One of the crucial agents in the transformation that occurred was William Little Lee, a friend of Charles Reed Bishop (who married the ali'i Bernice Pauahi, benefactress of the Kamehameha Schools). As a judge, then as chief justice of the Supreme Court, member of the Privy Council, and president of the Board of Commissioners to Quiet Land Titles, Lee was instrumental in shaping the legal and political institutions of his time in the image of the New England model that was native to him. He was, after all, a Harvard law graduate.

Lee was a man of worth and stature in the new political world he was helping to create. The following is an English translation of a passage that may describe Lee. It was written by Samuel M. Kamakau and appeared in the July 1, 1869, issue of *Ke Au Okoa*:

> A learned man had arrived with knowledge of the law, and the foreigners who were holding office in the government hastened to put him forward by saying how clever and learned he was and what good laws he would make for the Hawaiian people. The truth was, they were laws to change the old laws of the natives of the land and cause them to lick ti leaves like the dogs and gnaw bones thrown at the feet of strangers, while the strangers became their lords, and the hands and voices of strangers were raised over those of the native race. The commoners knew this and one and all expressed their disapproval and asked the king not to place foreigners in the offices of government lest the native race become a footstool for the foreigners. (Kamakau 1992A, 399)

The fear and foreboding contained in that passage were well-founded; we are still feeling the repercussions today.

Recently, the *Honolulu Advertiser* ran an article by historian Bob Dye that detailed the significant, participatory role that the first five trustees of the Bishop Estate played in the overthrow of the Hawaiian Kingdom. They were annexationists, one and all. This group comprised the following: First, Charles Reed Bishop whom I mentioned earlier as the friend of William Lee and the husband of Bernice Pauahi (he advocated annexation as early as 1853, if not earlier). Second, the Reverend Charles McEwen Hyde, a deeply racist Protestant minister who railed against Catholics, including Father Damien. Third, Charles Montague Cooke, son of missionary parents, and a teacher of Bernice Pauahi. Fourth, Samuel Mills Damon, to whom Bernice Pauahi willed the entire ahupuaʻa of Moanalua on the island of Oʻahu, consisting of some 7,000 acres. Fifth, and finally, William Owen Smith, also the son of missionary parents, and a trustee of the Lunalilo Estate in addition to the Bishop Estate.

Interestingly, except for Samuel Damon, the other four Bishop Estate Trustees also served as Trustees of Punahou School, which educated and groomed the sons and daughters of the haole elite to assume their places in a changing Hawaiʻi. At the same time, Principal William Oleson and Vice Principal Henry Townsend ran the Kamehameha Industrial School, established with Bernice Pauahi's money. Both men were members of the Hawaiian League, which was responsible, with the help of the Honolulu Rifles, for forcing the Bayonet Constitution on King Kalākaua—stripping away many of his powers and reducing him as much as possible to a figurehead.

This brings me back again to their contemporary, William Lee, who did a great deal to shape Hawaiian jurisprudence. The legal system established in the nineteenth century was used to disenfranchise Native Hawaiians in myriad ways, particularly with respect to land and water matters. It visited these effects on virtually every aspect of the life of the people.

Yet this same system, with its past and continuing history of abuses, can also be used as an effective tool to wage battle with the current political issues of our time. Perhaps it is no coincidence that I am married to a lawyer, who is originally from New England. Although I will say in his defense that he is trying to undo and reverse some of the harm created by William Lee and his professional descendants.

In my engagement with Hawaiian politics, I have found, almost without exception, that in order to resolve the most contentious issues, it has been necessary to work on multiple fronts. Legal forums, the courts, and administrative proceedings are as important as public hearings and protests.

My modest advice is: if a forum exists, participate in it, and if a forum doesn't exist, create it.

The Sunshine Law (Chapter 92) 21

TESTIMONY BEFORE THE
MAUI COUNTY COUNCIL ON SB 2127
FEBRUARY 16, 1994

I learned only this morning that there is an exact Senate version of a House bill that was killed two days ago. Senate Bill (SB) 2127 has not yet been heard by the Senate Committee on Government Operations, and it is my hope that the Council Committee of the Whole will not support SB 2127 for a number of reasons—only a few of which I can hurriedly point out.

Chapter 92 is one of the sterling laws of this state. Let me read from Hawai'i Revised Statutes Section 92-1, "The Declaration of Policy and Intent," which sets the tone for this law and governs all following sections.

> In a democracy, the people are vested with the ultimate decision-making power. Governmental agencies exist to aid the people in the formation and conduct of public policy. Opening up the governmental processes to public scrutiny and participation is the only viable and reasonable method of protecting the public's interest. Therefore, the legislation declares that it is the policy of this state that the formation and conduct of public policy—the discussions, deliberations, decisions, and action of governmental agencies—shall be conducted as openly as possible.

Adequate notice to the public in the form of "an agenda, which lists all of the items to be considered at [a] forthcoming meeting" is crucial to ensuring that governmental entities, including county councils, conduct their discussions, deliberations, decisions, and actions as openly as possible. Attorney General Opinion 85-2 reaffirms the necessity of specifying the subject matter of items listed on a public meeting agenda, further declaring that it is not sufficient to list broad categories of items.

Given this background, it would be against the open government policy of this state, and violative of the intent of the Sunshine Law, to amend Chapter 92 in the manner proposed by SB 2127. The bill states, in part, that:

> A county council may refer new business items to a Council committee if the referral occurs at a meeting for which notice was given as required under this section.

Such an amendment would allow any "new business" to be referred in the way described whether the item is a matter of minor importance or an issue of great interest to "a significant number of persons"; as might be the case, for instance, with zoning approval for a controversial golf course project. In cases like these, a county council less concerned about encouraging public participation and scrutiny could easily use the proposed revision of the Sunshine Law to reduce the number of occasions at which it would have to face the public and endure public testimony.

Chapter 92 protects an important public right by affording "all interested persons an opportunity to present oral testimony on any agenda item." SB 2127 seeks to eliminate one of the public's opportunities to testify through lack of notice regarding new business items. Simply put, if the public doesn't know that a particular item will be discussed or acted upon at a meeting, then the opportunity to testify will be lost.

A further question arises as to whether members of the public who happen to be present by chance at a meeting at which a previously unannounced new business item of interest is brought up would be allowed to testify on that item. The council may argue that since the particular new business item was not itself specifically noticed, it is not an agenda item and therefore is not subject to the open meeting provision of the Sunshine Law. Cloudy arguments of this sort would darken the sun of Chapter 92.

Nor is it at all clear when the council would be required to announce that its agenda will include a particular new business item for referral to committee. If, for instance, the specific new business item is not declared until after the public testimony portion of the council meeting has taken place (this council takes all public testimony at the very beginning of its meetings), the public would be effectively foreclosed from testifying on the item.

I can think of numerous cases in which it may serve the interests of particular council members to refer an item to committee without it first appearing on a properly noticed council agenda. It is difficult enough for the public to know about and participate in the workings of government as it is. Many of us rely upon a matter first appearing on the council's agenda for referral to committee as the earliest notice that the council will discuss a particular matter. The absence of this appearance would force the public to try to keep track of the eight council committee agendas in addition to the council's agenda. That would place an undue burden on the public and effectively restrict participation.

If the committee meeting or meetings are somehow missed by the public, that leaves only first and second reading approval as opportunities for public testimony. From a minimum of four opportunities to testify, it is conceivable that the public, lacking the current undiluted notice protections afforded by the Sunshine Law, would be reduced to two occasions for testimony—a reduction by half.

One last point: Section 10 of the council's present rules, titled "Order of Business," lists items "A" to "L." "New Business" is not even listed as an item. Of course the council is able to suspend its own rules on an affirmative vote of two-thirds of its entire membership; however, the signal it would send is that the council is intent on doing business with as little interference as possible from the public it is elected to serve—and heed.

However unpopular the views that members of the public may

express to this council from time to time, I humbly request that the council allow a true and unfettered democratic spirit to prevail in this chamber. After all, the First Amendment (which Chapter 92 affirms) is designed to protect not only the exercise of free speech but in particular the expression of unpopular views. That's the real test.

Ha'ikū Fire Station 22

BOARD OF VARIANCES AND APPEALS MEETING

JUNE 25, 2015

Good afternoon, board members. My name is Dana Naone Hall and I am testifying in support of a Petition to Intervene and Motion to Reconsider filed on my behalf.

Corporation counsel would have you deny my motions based on meeting a virtually impossible standard of notice for all but those living immediately adjacent to the project area or directly across Hāna Highway from the proposed project.

The county purchased the property in 2007. It took four years before a draft Environmental Assessment (EA) was prepared. I submitted timely comments on the EA in 2011. The environmental review process that precedes, by law, any other governmental approval and entitlement has not been completed. Therefore, the county is illegally implementing the Ha'ikū Fire Station project by obtaining approval for a variance from road-widening and shoulder improvements on a narrow, substandard road. It is important to note that the need for a variance was never disclosed in the draft EA. As a commenter on the draft EA I am entitled to a response from the preparer prior to the filing of a Finding of No Significant Impact or, as would be appropriate in this case, the filing of a Preparation Notice for an Environmental Impact Statement. In either case, I would not expect to be standing before you prior to the completion of the environmental review process. Nor would I have been expected to scour the classified ad section of the newspaper for the past four and a half years for a public notice on a variance for the Ha'ikū Fire Station.

Significant impacts would result from this project as currently planned. These impacts must be fully identified in a proper environmental document before we go any further. Piecemealing the approval process is only likely to result in longer delays to the project.

The Salt of Kūʻau 23

TESTIMONY BEFORE THE MAUI COUNTY COUNCIL PLANNING COMMITTEE ON THE PAIA-HAIKU COMMUNITY PLAN

MARCH 9, 1994

Good evening. I am one of the housewives who served on the Paia-Haiku Citizens Advisory Committee.

Let me begin by saying that I recently came across an article authored by Committee Chair Junior Moniz in a Hawaiʻi realtor magazine. This article outlines Mr. Moniz's philosophy about the virtues of the current council and gives us some of his ideas on planning. As someone who is often called an activist on behalf of Hawaiian, community, and environmental issues, I must say that what struck me about the article and Committee Chair Moniz's other public pronouncements is that the chair is also an activist. Perhaps it takes one to recognize one. Mr. Moniz's activism, however, is solidly on behalf of development interests.

Mr. Moniz apparently believes that assigning a less intensive designation in a community plan to property whose current zoning would allow a more intensive use should not be allowed. In this view of planning, property cannot be down-zoned once it attains a particular zoning—no matter how inappropriate that zoning may prove to be over time.

But excuse me, Mr. Moniz, I don't mean to single you out. You are after all one member of a self-proclaimed majority on the council. My plea is to all of the members of this committee and extends

Isaac Hall and Dana Naone Hall sitting among the waterworn boulders of Pilale Bay.
Photograph by Kapulani Landgraf.

to the entire council to adopt the community plan update developed by the Paia-Haiku Citizens Advisory Committee. Others have spoken to you of the balanced perspective that our citizens advisory committee brought to its review of the plan. In this undertaking we were ably assisted by the planning department.

In the end, of course, the council will be the final arbiter in this round of decision-making. What we are all asking ourselves is who will the council bestow its approval upon? I am speaking of the majority of the council, which will influence the actions of this committee. I am not speaking of those individual members who show from time to time a conscience about what it means to be a public servant. I am speaking of those council members for whom the idea and ideal of what it means to be a public servant appears to be a foreign notion.

Please believe me that we want to encourage you to do what is right for our region. You have the opportunity to reflect the will of the people tonight. I urge you to do so, and end by saying:

> I come before you with the salt of Kūʻau on me
> I come to you from the wind and waves at Hoʻokipa
> from the waters of Hoʻolawa
> and the depths of Māliko and Kikipi
> from Kauhikoa and Kuiaha
> to Ulumalu and Pilale
>
> Living on Maui we look to Hāna in the east
> where the sun rises
> and from our beautiful coastline
> we look toward the west
> where the sun sets beyond
> the burial places of our ancestors
>
> We stand in the protective shadow of Haleakalā
> where do you stand?

Connections with Past Remain Today

24

LETTER TO THE EDITOR OF THE *MAUI NEWS*

SUNDAY, MARCH 28, 1988

Ordinarily, I am a happy reader of the *Maui News*. The reporting of events, people, and issues that affect Maui County is, for the most part, solid and worthy of praise. However, the editorial, titled "Hoʻokipa's Beauty Can Be Improved," that appeared in the March 4 edition of the paper deserves a less praiseworthy response.

Hawaiian speakers, at a public meeting held to discuss proposed improvements for Hoʻokipa Park, had urged that great care be taken so that the bones of those buried in the sand dunes along that remarkably beautiful length of coast would not be disturbed. The editorial's answer to this concern (unlike the receptive manner in which testimony was received by Parks Director Marilyn Moniz-Kahoohanohano that evening) was disturbingly callous. The less quick we are as a society to disturb the graves of "earlier populations," the less often we will have to invoke the facile statements of the editorial that "the land and its beauty and usefulness belong to the living." As if that in itself confers on us the right to do as we please while excusing us of our deeper responsibilities.

It's clear to me that the writer of the editorial has little idea of what it would actually, and by this I mean practically, take to treat ancestral bones deliberately uncovered by the activities of the living with reverence. At the meeting, the call was for as little grading as possible in the sandy soil makai of the road that winds through the park. The speakers, with extensive knowledge of Hawaiian culture and Hawaiian burials, knew what they were talking about. The cost and time involved with careful archaeological excavation of human burials at Hoʻokipa could well prove to be prohibitive—as well as unnecessary.

It would, of course, be easier to scoop up whole areas with a bulldozer, but I trust that the definition of reverent treatment alluded to would not be stretched as far as that. The park can and will be improved, and the improvements can occur in such a way that cultural and spiritual concerns are respected at the same time.

I must also take issue with the assertion that "not every ancient burial site is a historic one." Again, this is a convenient way of dismissing what is there in order to destroy it. Recent battles between Hawaiian cultural interests and the interests of developers have been joined over precisely this point. If a developer is successful in convincing the governmental permit-granting bodies and agencies that a site is not "significant," it means almost certain destruction of the site and a green light for the developer.

When the debate over significance is more difficult to resolve, politically and legally, as in the case of Hui Alanui o Mākena's desire to protect Mākena Road, the battle can wax long indeed. At times, significance has been narrowly interpreted to mean only those sites currently listed on either the National or Hawaiʻi Registers of Historic Places. This does not take into account the numberless sites that have yet to be identified or ones that have not been properly surveyed and nominated to a historical register. (Nor does listing on either register, in itself, guarantee that a site will be preserved.)

No doubt the debate will continue. But rather than continue it in an argumentative fashion, I would prefer to describe significance in Hawaiian cultural terms, as expressed by the example of Mākena Road—and hope that this moʻolelo, or story, sheds some light on the matter.

Four hundred years ago, the Hawaiʻi aliʻi ʻUmialīloa advised the Maui chief Kihaapiʻilani to undertake a project that would benefit the people. Kihaapiʻilani's response was to build a road that circled the island of Maui.

It gives me a deep and abiding pleasure to write the words "four hundred years ago" in order to relate a story from the long tradition of our people, and it gives me a deep and abiding sense of belonging to this place when I walk or drive on the sections of Alaloa, attributed to Kihaapiʻilani, that still exist today. I think of those whose names are no longer known to us, who shaped and fixed in place on steep slopes the ancient road, and who walked before me on the sandy dunes carrying nets and gourds full of water.

We are continually imagining the past, what it was like for our ancestors fifty years, ninety years ago, more than a thousand years ago. Sometimes the past is made visible, as in the presence of the old road, and our use of the road is a way of preserving a link to an older part of ourselves and keeping open a way of being in the future.

In the same way, the ancient welcome of Hoʻokipa extends to all of us. May we be as hospitable in our response.

Paʻa ke Kahua

25

Even in these difficult times when economic interests exert a seemingly all-powerful hand in what happens to our islands, it is still possible to claim places where our culture can revive and the spirits of our ancestors and their iwi can rest undisturbed. Honokahua, a place of endings, was the beginning of my efforts to protect burial sites—a lifelong task to help make firm the foundation from which we can continue to grow and thrive as a people.

A CALLING AT HONOKAHUA

The disturbance and disinterment of more than a thousand Native Hawaiian burials at Honokahua might easily have been the subject of after-the-fact speculation and rumor, and might never have garnered statewide attention and the recognition that unmarked burials required protection, if chance or fate had not made it possible for Isaac Hall and me to be in attendance at the last Maui County Planning Commission meeting of the year on December 19, 1986.

We were present that day for another agenda item when someone else at the meeting mentioned that a planning department staff member had reported to the commission earlier that a section of the Piʻilani Trail had been identified on shoreline land where Maui Land and Pineapple Company, through its subsidiary Kapalua Land Company, planned to build a luxury hotel. The staff report also referred to a burial site.

By then, we and Hui Alanui o Mākena (Hui) were more than two years into the conflict with Seibu (a Japanese corporation whose owner, Yoshiaki Tsutsumi, *Forbes* magazine deemed at that time the richest man in the world) over its planned closure of the old Mākena Road, which had evolved over time from the Pi'ilani Trail. Isaac addressed the commission before it voted on the Special Management Area (SMA) permit, the final discretionary permit for development in shoreline areas. He asked the commission to defer action on the permit until the Hui had a chance to review and comment on the information submitted. The commission did not hesitate to grant the permit.

Shortly thereafter, we obtained a copy of the archaeological report containing information about the burial site and trail. The burial site was identified by archaeologists in the late 1960s from human skeletal remains eroding out of the partially lithified dune behind the beach. The Honokahua burial site was placed on the Hawai'i Register of Historic Places, then removed in the 1970s, along with numerous other significant sites, because a State Attorney General Opinion determined that landowners must first be notified and approve any listing.

Our first visit with the Hui to Honokahua occurred in January 1987. The shoreline dune consisted of two connected sand formations—an upper dune and a lower dune. Fragmented human skeletal remains were visible on the dune surface among the weedy plants and sparse grasses—evidence of the effects of recent activities by a stable operation, as well as disturbance caused by transient campsites. A historic period dump also impinged on a portion of the dune.

We left Honokahua with the feeling that something more needed to be done. A review of the hotel development plans revealed that the entire dune (and, consequently, all the burials in it—an unknown number at that time) would be removed. An underground basement and parking garage were planned for the lower dune, and the new lobby of the hotel would displace the stepping-stone trail on the upper dune.

A Motion for Reconsideration of the planning commission's

decision to grant the SMA permit was prepared by Isaac, and a hearing on the motion was set for February 20, 1987. In the few weeks before the hearing, the Hui informed members of the community and solicited the support of the Office of Hawaiian Affairs (OHA).

The hearing took place in the fluorescent-lit Civil Defense Conference Room before nine commissioners—none of whom were Hawaiian. Every speaker, with the exception of Kapalua Land Company president Colin Cameron and his attorney, spoke eloquently for preservation of the burial site and trail and against the granting of the permit. In the end, only the commissioner representing the island of Lānaʻi voted in our favor, stating that he had learned more about Hawaiian culture that day than at any other time in his life.

Sorrowful as the commission's adverse decision was—the mood following the meeting was black and thunderous—I felt, inexplicably, that we had not been defeated, that Hawaiian people had spoken up to protect the graves of their ancestors and that somehow, someday there would be a cataclysmic shift. I had no reason to feel this way, but perhaps in stepping forward and speaking up we had reconnected to our ancestors in a fundamental way.

Aunty Alice Kuloloio had said with regard to the Hui's struggles with Seibu, "We are nothing. We are like the dust." Rather than feeling diminished, I took her words to mean that Seibu, with all the power and money at its disposal (not to speak of government support), had everything. We, on the other hand, had nothing and, therefore, had nothing to lose. Only Seibu had something to lose. Being like the dust freed us to act with imagination and conviction. I have attempted to do so when working on myriad issues, believing that this is one of the ways in which we keep the culture fresh and relevant to our time.

Because the Hui had pressed so adamantly for the protection of the burial site, the commission, without irony, in its only concession to the concerns raised, issued a decision in which the Hui was invited to develop "sensitive" disinterment and reinterment plans for the burials at Honokahua, along with the State Historic Preservation Officer—who is also the chair of the Board of Land and Natural

Resources, Kapalua Land Company, and OHA. The Hui was faced with a daunting dilemma. How could it participate in devising the conditions under which the very burials it had sought to protect were dug up? The thrust of the testimony had been that there was nothing inherently sensitive about disinterment.

It could appear that the commission's proposed sop to Hawaiian feelings and beliefs wasn't much of a dilemma at all. Washing one's hands of the whole enterprise and walking away was an option elected by some of the earliest participants with a departing retort that the hewa was on those who dug up the iwi. For the Hui, it was not so simple, and, as the crisis of conscience deepened, the kūpuna buried in the Honokahua dune made their presence known.

Six weeks after the commission hearing, on the Friday before Easter in April, two members of our group headed to Honokahua for a late day visit. One of the men had been stirred to prepare ho'okupu for the kūpuna. He had been feeling their presence for weeks and now he knew he had to gather four specific items—one was kalo, which he cooked for the first time in his life (it was also his first ho'okupu), and another was kapa, because the kūpuna were cold. He said he did not hear voices or see spirits, rather he expressed his connection as one of understanding what the kūpuna were feeling.

What transpired after they arrived, beginning with a dark cloud forming over Moloka'i and quickly advancing to the northwestern coast of Maui where they sat below the dune, put a definitive end to the dilemma about whether or not to participate in developing procedures for the disinterment plan. The kūpuna had shown themselves and we could not ignore what was about to happen to them. If anything, we had a duty to be there to comfort them and to bear witness to the coming acts of desecration.

We entered into several months of discussion and negotiation, which occurred, for the most part, between the contract archaeologist for Kapalua Land Company and the Hui. Our primary position, from which we never wavered, was that the burial site should be protected and preserved, not dug up. Lacking the power to impose our point of view on the other parties, we turned our attention to limiting the amount of disturbance that would occur to the iwi kupuna, especially with regard to osteological examinations, and to assure that any moepū, grave goods, found with specific individuals would be reburied together with those same individuals.

We had no example to go by. Instead, we had to think deeply and feel our way around problems, guided by the overriding desire to reduce wherever possible additional harm to the kūpuna. It later turned out that the resolutions of many of the thorny issues we puzzled over (before arriving at a way to handle them) constituted the precursor thinking necessary to—and later incorporated in—Hawai'i's burial law, Chapter 6E-43. But that was several years away.

After a Memorandum of Agreement (MOA) was executed between the four parties (the state, Kapalua, OHA, Hui), disinterment commenced in August 1987 with a small crew of archaeologists. With the terms of the MOA as a framework, strict control was exercised over the manner in which the burials were recovered and transported to a temporary storage facility. The archaeological supervisor in charge of field operations for the project was meticulous and proved over time to be an ally rather than a nemesis. She was always forthcoming with information, and on my numerous trips to the site, I learned a great deal about archaeology, traditional burials, and burial practices, albeit under dire circumstances.

The quiet, unhurried pace began to quicken as the months went by and the size of the crew grew in number. The MOA required a careful series of steps, which made the disinterments costly and time-consuming. Nevertheless, the burials continued to be extracted one by one. By August 1988, a year later, Kapalua executives were becoming increasingly concerned over whether construction could be initiated within the two-year deadline required by the SMA permit. In order to meet the deadline, they decided to focus on completing disinterment of the lower dune, while erecting a barrier between the upper and lower dune, which would allow pile-driving to commence on the lower dune area, satisfying the permit condition. Kapalua began seeking approval for its plan.

The Hui vigorously opposed Kapalua's proposed plan during an

Maui people gathered to contemplate and reflect on the disturbance of hundreds of iwi kupuna at Honokahua in late 1988.

Photograph from the author's collection.

incendiary meeting at which a Ritz-Carlton official was also present. The Hui reiterated that the disinterment of the dune was wrong to begin with and that if Kapalua could not follow the MOA, it should stop the digging altogether. To back up our brave words, I flew to Moloka'i, where the OHA board was meeting, to seek the trustees' support of our position. If OHA could be convinced, it would make it more difficult for the state, another signatory of the agreement, to side with Kapalua and, at a minimum, the issue would be stalemated. The trustees, after ample persuasion and confronted with the mounting number of burials (now more than several hundred), agreed with our position.

Word began to circulate more widely about what was happening at Honokahua. Pualani Kanahele was teaching at Maui Community College at the time. Enrolled in one of her classes, I informed her of the increasing number of burials being excavated. A letter to the editor written by Edward Kanahele, Pua's husband, who later founded Hui Mālama I Nā Kūpuna O Hawai'i Nei, was published in one of the Honolulu dailies, calling attention to the ongoing disinterment. The media became much more active in reporting on Honokahua and, as activity at the burial site accelerated (the initial crew of fewer than five working at the site ballooned to more than eighty before the digging was finally halted), so did statewide interest.

Before Honokahua, thousands upon thousands of Hawaiian burials had been routinely dug up since the arrival of the missionaries in 1820. Disturbing and displacing Native Hawaiian iwi was not new. What differentiated Honokahua was a drawn-out excavation process that occurred over many months, not a quick unearthing and scattering witnessed by a few. It provided the time necessary for people to comprehend the magnitude of what was happening and, most importantly, to reflect on the spiritual and moral dimensions of such actions. Once the reality of Honokahua pierced the public conscience, the digging had to stop.

The rest of this story is well-documented. People in Hawai'i were galvanized by Honokahua. In December, Governor John Waihe'e stepped in to stop the digging and conduct a reassessment. Maui's

Mayor Hannibal Tavares joined in the effort. There remained a number of steps before final resolution of the controversy, but the changes wrought by Honokahua were monumental—on a personal level and in terms of expanding protection to burial sites through the adoption of Hawai'i's burial law in 1990. Significantly, this expansion of historic preservation law in Hawai'i provides a deliberative regulatory framework for determining whether to preserve in place or relocate unmarked buried human skeletal remains.

Twenty-three years later, implementation of the burial law has weakened and the law is being distorted by interpretations that divest island burial councils of their proper jurisdiction, thereby denying burial sites and the places where they are found the protection they deserve. While the current situation is regrettable, it can be corrected. The iwi of our ancestors are planted in the land. We exist and flourish because they exist. Honokahua still calls, and we must answer that call today.

Published in *I Ulu I Ka 'Āina: Land*, ed. Jonathan K. Osorio (Honolulu: University of Hawai'i Press, 2014), 39–44.,

Maui Planning Commission Special Meeting 26

MAUI COUNTY CIVIL DEFENSE CONFERENCE ROOM

FEBRUARY 20, 1987

Testimony against a Special Management Area Use Permit and Step I Planned Development approvals for the Kapalua Village Hotel and in support of motions: (a) for reconsideration, (b) to reopen the docket and take further evidence, (c) to vacate order for lack of adequate notice, (d) to intervene, (e) to require EA and EIS, and (f) to waive rules.

Good morning, commissioners. My name is Dana Naone Hall. I would like to begin by correcting some of the misinformation contained in the memoranda filed by attorneys for Maui Land and Pineapple Company and Mid-Continental Development.

I am not the president of Hui Alanui o Mākena. Nowhere on affidavits or public records of any kind does this designation appear. We have no president. I am just a member.

I did not begin receiving the agendas for planning commission meetings in my name until January of this year, contrary to what is stated in the memoranda. The agendas that I was privy to in 1986 arrived in the mail, several times toward the end of the year, a day or two after the hearings listed on the agenda were held. I did not, and Hui Alanui o Mākena did not, receive any direct notice of the hearing on the Kapalua permit.

It is curious to me that counsel for the applicant states so unequivocally that I received the commission agenda. Is the mailing list kept by the planning department open to scrutiny by anyone demanding to see it?

I am frequently in the planning department, but no one has ever alerted me to the fact that the Honokahua Burial Site and a section of the Piʻilani Trail or Alaloa would be the subject of—and subjected to—Maui Land and Pineapple's development plans for the Kapalua Village Hotel. Had I known, I would have certainly informed other members of the Hui, and we would have moved to ask for intervention in a timely way. We would certainly have testified at the hearings. Hui Alanui o Mākena is well-known for its efforts to preserve and protect the Piʻilani Trail wherever it is located. The Planning Department and its staff are in no doubt of this, and our members have stated this position publicly many times.

With respect to the notice that the commission published on the public hearings for the permit in the *Honolulu Advertiser* and the *Maui News*, the notice states only that:

> Consultants on behalf of Mid-Continental Development Inc. and Maui Land and Pineapple Company Inc. request an SMA permit in order to develop a 450-room hotel and related improvements near Honokahua Bay, TMK 4-2-01:35 and portions of 5, 18 and 31, Kapalua, Maui.

There is nothing in that bare announcement to alert anyone in the public to the existence of the Honokahua Burial Site and a portion of the Piʻilani Trail, which the hotel project has targeted for removal and desecration.

Counsel for the applicant has claimed repeatedly that "ample consideration" was given by the planning commission to the matters before it and that there are no grounds for reopening this case.

I read carefully the minutes of the public hearings on November 18 and the continuance of the hearing on December 19. Between the two hearings, a total of one person, who happens to operate the bar and grill at Kapalua, testified. The commission itself did not discuss the archaeological and cultural sites that are at issue today.

There were discussions about employee housing benefits, the zoning for the adjoining parcel, visual corridors to the ocean, housing requirements for resort and commercial areas, the bypass road, the opening of the West Maui airport, carpooling for employees, and the like, but not one word about what concerns us here: the desecration and destruction of a prehistoric burial site and a section of the Alaloa that circled Maui.

Although the December 19 staff report to the planning commission identified these sites, the recommendation was that they did not warrant preservation and would be adequately disposed of by "data recording" or what is also called "documentary construction monitoring." This is a callous and very cold way of treating Native Hawaiian burials, a method that anyone else in this room of another culture would shudder at if it were applied to their ancestors.

The fact that there was no discussion by the commission on the subject of these sites suggests not that ample consideration was given, but that no consideration was given. This is an oversight that the commission can now correct by reopening this case, and allowing the intervention of Hui Alanui o Mākena and other Hawaiians who are deeply concerned about the further proposed destruction of what remains of our culture.

The conclusion of the December 19 staff report, which is based on the analysis contained in the report, lists twelve separate issues—none of which mention the archaeological and cultural sites, making it clear that these sites were not adequately considered.

Finally, if the applicant, Maui Land and Pineapple, is allowed to bury the concerns we have raised before the commission on the protection and preservation of significant historic and prehistoric cultural sites, then they will have made a clear point to the community that truly nothing is sacred.

Leinani Sakamoto and Leahi Hall offer ho'okupu at Honokahua as OHA trustee Manu Kahaiali'i (left) *and Kula Kaiapuni o Maui students and families* (right) *look on during a ceremony in February 1989.*
Photograph by Ed Tanji.

Letter to William Paty, State Historic Preservation Officer, Opposition to Further Osteological Examination of Iwi At Honokahua 27

JUNE 16, 1989

Dear Mr. Paty:

Hui Alanui o Mākena (Hui) is opposed to further osteological examination of Native Hawaiians disinterred at Honokahua. Our primary concern continues to be the protection of the burials from further disturbance.

The Hui and the Office of Hawaiian Affairs (OHA) made it clear that participation in the Memorandum of Agreement (MOA) with Kapalua Land Company and the State Historic Preservation Office did not confer approval on the decision to disinter. The MOA imposed additional standards and conditions should disinterment occur; however, the position of the Native Hawaiian signatories has consistently been for preservation of the site and against disinterment.

We were not successful in effecting a reconsideration of the decision to disinter until late last year. At that time, with public opinion strongly stirred against continued disinterment and in keeping with the universal recognition of the sanctity of burial places, Governor John Waiheʻe called for cessation of the disinterment. Subsequently, Kapalua Land Company voluntarily agreed to stop archaeological digging at the Honokahua site.

It has been the Hui's understanding, as an original signatory to the MOA, that the standards and conditions imposed on the archaeological, including osteological, work at Honokahua were linked to the previously approved decision to disinter. Once the decision to disinter was reversed, secondary or other agreements and conditions were no longer in effect.

In essence, the Honokahua issue has come full circle. In letters to Maui County Planning director Christopher Hart dated February 3, 1987, and February 19, 1987, from State Parks administrator Ralston Nagata (when the Hui had first requested reconsideration and review of the Special Management Area permit granted to Kapalua Land Company), comments from the Department of Land and Natural Resources (Department) included suggested mitigation measures for the Honokahua Burial Site. These measures, contained in the letter of February 3, pp. 2–3, are as follows:

> Whenever practical, in reviewing a development Project, we encourage the preservation of sites that fulfill multiple criteria such as T-4 and 1342 [Honokahua Burial Site] especially when the development can incorporate such sites into their designs for public appreciation interpretation purposes.
>
> Burials are somewhat different. Realizing that these are sensitive sites, not appropriate for interpretation, *we recommend to developers that they get public input to help the developer determine whether in-place preservation is a viable alternative to sensitive disinterment/data recovery.* (Emphasis added)

They are further clarified in the letter of February 19, p. 2:

> 2. The Burial site. Again, in practice over the last 2 years, early in planning stages, we point out to developers that burials are sensitive sites, and *we urge developers to consider public input prior to determining whether preservation in-place or respectful reinterment/data recovery is the more viable alternative.* The minimal recommended level for mitigation is again archaeological data recovery and respectful reinterment or archiving of skeletal material. (Emphasis added)

The developer's original decision was for the "minimal recommended level for mitigation" in the form of archaeological data recovery and respectful reinterment. The decision has been reversed due to increased public input, and preservation in place is now the more viable alternative.

At present, a task force appointed by Maui Mayor Hannibal Tavares is developing a mitigation plan for the Honokahua Burial Site that involves reinterment of the burials, in their original approximate locations, and the restoration and preservation of the site.

Section 6E-43 of the Hawai'i Revised Statutes mandates the preparation of a mitigation plan for significant remains. However, Subsection (3) goes on to state:

> If this plan calls for data recovery, and the removal of the burials is warranted, then archaeological analysis must occur, along with appropriate study of the remains by a qualified physical anthropologist. If lineal descendants can be identified by the department, and if they oppose the physical anthropological study, then it shall not occur.

The reinterment and restoration plan being prepared by the mayor's task force does not include data recovery. Clearly the removal of the burials is no longer warranted. Thus, the requirement for "appropriate study of the remains by a qualified physical anthropologist" is not triggered.

Even if the study requirement is applicable, it may be fairly argued that "appropriate study" has already been conducted on the Honokahua iwi. It should be noted that basic osteological data was collected for every burial removed from the Honokahua site. Field burial forms (filled out by either the field director or the crew supervisor) and skeletal inventory forms (filled out by field osteologists) recorded essential archaeological data.

In terms of osteological data, this included information about age and sex (except for prepubescent individuals), and readily apparent pathologies, as well as epigenetic traits. The actual removal of the burials was performed by or with the direction of the field osteologists and trained assistants. Photographs of the burials were also taken in the field; these form an important pictorial record that can be referred to in the future.

Contrary to the representations made in a letter from Terry Hunt, president of the Society for Hawaiian Archaeology, to Governor Waiheʻe, dated April 27, 1989, the osteological expertise in the field made it possible to identify nearly all of the individuals disinterred at Honokahua, except, for instance, in extreme cases of bone scatter. Although some nonhuman bones were found with the burials, there was no mistaking of dog bones for human ones. Given the high standards of the fieldwork at the Honokahua site, respectful and sensitive reburial can be accomplished.

In addition, approximately two-thirds of the 920 burials exhumed have undergone further osteological analysis in the laboratory. Before this analysis was discontinued several months ago, some selective analysis was conducted to enable a more representative skeletal sampling of the site. At question is not whether there should be a ban on any osteological analysis—since, as has been previously stated, some analysis has been conducted on all identified burials—but how *much* more analysis should be allowed. It is the Hui's position that the "appropriate study" requirement has been fulfilled.

Now that reinterment is about to begin, it would be highly inappropriate to retain the Honokahua bones solely for the purpose of continued study; the dominant cultural sentiment is for immediate reburial. The one- to two-year period that would be required to satisfy certain scientific requirements (with respect to access to the bones for the checking and cross-checking of data) is also impractical given Kapalua Land Company's intention to proceed with the development of the Ritz-Carlton hotel. Although the hotel is proposed for an area mauka of the burial site, the site still remains a part of the overall hotel project.

Finally, lineal descendants have opposed osteological study of the ancestral bones at Honokahua. Hui member Ron Makaula Dela Cruz has stated both his lineal connection to the Honokahua burials and his opposition to further osteological analysis. Other members of the Native Hawaiian families who trace their descendancy from the Honokahua area over many generations have also been identified and have publicly objected to osteological analysis.

These objections to osteological analysis are rooted in the culture of Native Hawaiians, who continue to respect potent traditional admonitions about the desecration and disturbance of ancestral bones. Lack of respect for one's ancestors is directly linked to "exposing their bones for all to see" (Pukui 1983, 225, 174).

As Kawena Pukui further notes: "It is with the bones (iwi) that the ʻuhane remained identified . . . therefore the bones . . . must be kept safe from molestation" (Handy and Pukui 1989, 151).

The more mana (spiritual power) a person possessed, the more sought after the bones would be for fishhooks or other uses by which the mana imbued in the bones could be drawn on. Particular care and secrecy surrounded the burial or disposition of aliʻi bones, but commoners also took care that the bones of their families and ancestors be spared disturbance and disinterment by others. This could not always be prevented, but even at a site as large as Honokahua there is no evidence of large-scale prehistoric manmade disturbance of the site (later burials that were found to have broken through earlier burials may have been, in a number of cases, inadvertent). A review of primary ethnographic literature bears out these essential points.

More importantly, cultural values as basic as those having to do with regard and respect for the dead are more aptly conveyed as part of the ongoing oral tradition (rather than as a tenet of a written creed). These ancient human feelings that live on in us today are an unbroken connection to a time in our deepest past and to the primordial gods, as we are the connection to future generations. Arguments about the greater public good cannot be interposed to sever us from the spiritual responsibility that we bear to our ancestors and to our living heritage.

Sincerely,
Dana Naone Hall

OHA board chair Thomas Kaulukukui Sr. executing the Honokahua Burial Site Agreement while Dana Naone Hall waits to sign for Hui Alanui o Mākena. Also present but not pictured were Leslie Kuloloio and Charles Maxwell.
Photograph from the author's collection.

Remarks Delivered at the Groundbreaking of the Ritz-Carlton, Kapalua

28

DECEMBER 4, 1990

Thank you for this opportunity to reflect once again on endings and beginnings. What began in discord four years ago has presented us with another occasion for deepening our understanding of this place and strengthening our relation to the land and to each other. As I mentioned, for Hawaiians, Kapalua will always represent an ending and a beginning.

The iwi, the bones of our ancestors, lie at Honokahua, the end of physical life, but the spirit of our ancestors continues to guide us. It is because we are able to preserve the physical elements of bone and sand dune that there will be a continuation and a new beginning for all of us.

So you see that reverence for our ancestors is the same as a reverence for the place, and the protection of Honokahua is evidence of our continuity in this place. It is as the name indicates—a foundation. It is also a place of vision.

The Cameron family, the state of Hawai'i, Mayor Hannibal Tavares, and many others have helped to assure the continuity I speak of by recognizing the essential identity of Honokahua. The ancient and the modern exist side by side at Honokahua.

This coexistence is necessary for all of our endeavors. To Maui Land and Pineapple Company, Nissho Iwai, and the Ritz-Carlton, we wish you well. May your foundation be strong.

(Left to right) *Rene Sylva, Dana Naone Hall, and Lehua Pali stand near the edge of a backhoe trench that exposed a buried wall in the Waihe'e Sand Dune. The tall white pole in the background marks the location of a feature of the proposed golf course.*
Photograph by Masako Cordray.

Archaeological Conference Talk 29

HISTORIC HAWAI'I FOUNDATION

WAILEA, 1990

Usually at conferences of this nature, in the past few years, I have found myself in the role of the bad fairy—bearing news of already troubled situations and portending future conflicts with the state, the county, and developers over historical and cultural preservation issues. As an example, at the last conference on Maui sponsored by the Historic Hawai'i Foundation, in which I participated, the Honokahua Burial Site issue was just beginning to receive widespread attention in the state. The resolution of the Honokahua conflict was several months away and no one knew then what shape that resolution would take.

It has now been almost exactly a year and one month since the state of Hawai'i, the Office of Hawaiian Affairs (OHA), Kapalua Land Company, and Hui Alanui o Mākena, a group of which I am a member, signed the Honokahua Burial Site Agreement. In the intervening year since the signing of the agreement, a great deal has occurred with respect to historic preservation that may be of interest to this audience. A great deal of good, I might add, but in order to give the rest of my brief talk a proper context, allow me to describe some of the particulars of the Honokahua issue for those who may not know or who may have forgotten the details.

Kapalua Land Company was granted a Special Management

Area (SMA) permit for a proposed hotel on a 13.6-acre parcel located along the shoreline of Makāluapuna Point and Honokahua Bay within what is now the Kapalua Resort. Hui Alanui o Mākena challenged the granting of the SMA permit by the Maui County Planning Commission because sections of the Pi'ilani Trail—a trail that at one time circled the entire island of Maui—had been identified on the property and an archaeological survey had also confirmed the presence of an undetermined number of prehistoric burials. Plans for the proposed hotel located the lobby in the area of the trail, and underground parking and massive footings for the foundation would necessitate excavation of the entire sand dune in the project area.

The Hui was unsuccessful in its attempt to persuade the planning commission to reconsider the grant of the permit, and in order not to abandon the burials altogether, the Hui, along with OHA, the state of Hawai'i through its Historic Preservation Officer, and Kapalua Land Company, entered into an agreement that specifically detailed the manner in which burials would be disinterred. At the time, the Memorandum of Agreement was the most specific of its kind as it related to the disinterment of burials.

Among other conditions, the agreement stated that any artifacts or burial goods found in the course of excavation would be reinterred at another location along with the skeletal remains disinterred from the dune.

Excavations at the site began on August 11, 1987. By mid-October of 1988, 791 individuals had been disinterred at Honokahua and a minimum of 60 additional individuals had been identified from scattered bone material collected at the site. In the next two months the Honokahua issue came to a head, so to speak, with protests and the intervention of Governor Waihe'e and Mayor Tavares. When the disinterment ceased, approximately 1,000 individuals had been recovered, and it is estimated that approximately 1,000 more individuals remained undisturbed at the site, safe from further disinterment.

As troubling and distressful as the Honokahua Burial Site issue was to Hawaiians and many others in the state, what has come of the increased awareness Honokahua brought about is worthy of note. The state of Hawai'i purchased a preservation and conservation easement for the 13.6-acre parcel, in effect buying the development rights to the land, and the signing of the Honokahua Burial Site Agreement mentioned earlier brought many of the legalities concerning the site to a conclusion.

During negotiations regarding the Honokahua site, Colin Cameron stated that what he and his partners sought in the resolution of the issue was to be "made whole" again. I might add that our cultural desire as Hawaiians paralleled that economic desire, and by the end of April of this year the site was made whole again with the reinterment of the iwi.

Legislation that would afford better protection for prehistoric burials through the amendment of Chapter 6E, our state's Historic Preservation Laws, was introduced in the 1989 session. Although the proposed legislation was not passed by the '89 legislature, Mr. William Paty, the head of the Department of Land and Natural Resources (DLNR) and the State Historic Preservation Officer, announced that his department would set up five island burial councils to assist DLNR in making determinations about the proper course of action regarding future prehistoric burial issues. These burial councils include one for the island of Hawai'i, one for the island of O'ahu, a council for the islands of Kaua'i and Ni'ihau, and in Maui County a Lāna'i island representative sits with the Maui council while Moloka'i has a separate council. To date, the councils have served in an advisory capacity to the Historic Sites Section, now the Historic Preservation Division, of the DLNR.

In the next month, the councils will be formally organized to comport with a burial bill introduced in the 1990 legislature and signed into law by Governor Waihe'e on July 3. This bill is a successor to the one introduced a year earlier. The governor will appoint representatives from the Hawaiian community as well as representatives of development and large landowner interests to participate as members of the five island councils.

A primary difference between the councils convened by DLNR in 1989 and the councils that will be established through the amendment of Chapter 6E is that the new councils will have the authority to determine the preservation or relocation of previously identified Native Hawaiian burial sites. In the case of an inadvertent discovery of a burial site, the law remains the same, with the DLNR determining whether the human skeletal remains will be relocated or remain in place. The island councils will be notified of all discoveries of Hawaiian burials.

The operative difference is that the island burial councils will have primary decision-making powers over previously identified burials—in other words, burials whose existence is known, including those identified in archaeological surveys and in a development project's planning process, while DLNR will exercise primary decision-making over inadvertent, unknown, or unsuspected burials, in consultation with the appropriate burial council. An appeals process is also a part of the new legislation, allowing for the appeal of any decision made by the island councils. The appeals panel would be composed of three island burial council chairs, three Board of Land and Natural Resources (BLNR) members, and the BLNR chair.

This significant piece of legislation is the direct result of what occurred at Honokahua with the uncovering of the site and its second and final sealing, emphasizing one interpretation of the name Kapalua as "twice covered." I share in the deep satisfaction of the many people who helped to bring about the particular resolution at Honokahua and the more generalized and far-reaching protection that is afforded all prehistoric burial sites through the new legislation.

Before I leave the subject of burials, I'd like to touch on two other burial issues that have arisen since Honokahua. The first involves what is referred to as a remnant sand dune at Wai'ehu two miles outside of Wailuku. This remnant dune is located on a relatively narrow band of land between Kahekili Highway on the mauka side and the state's housing project on the makai or sea side. Steady urbanization of that area of Waiehu has whittled down what was once a large Pleistocene period dune formation to a finger of sand.

Wailuku Agribusiness and C. Brewer Properties planned to mine the dune for sand, reducing the dune from more than 80 feet high at its peak to road level. The mining and selling of the sand would contribute substantial income to the property owners, and it would also provide a level area for ten proposed housing units as part of C. Brewer's plan for the Piihana Project District.

To compress this story, after several meetings with the Maui/Lāna'i Island Burial Council, during which the participants discussed various proposals, the companies involved agreed to abandon initial plans that would have substantially reduced the dune and instead proposed to reduce the dune to a three-to-one grade (the minimum county grade is two-to-one—for every foot dug, a 2-foot bench or flat surface is required). A three-to-one grade would present a gentler, sloped appearance while preserving most of the dune feature on the property. This was an acceptable resolution of the matter theoretically, but the dune itself had the final say.

A major reason that C. Brewer and Wailuku Agribusiness decided not to go forward with plans to drastically reduce the dune was because of the likelihood that the dune would contain human burials. During the three-to-one grading process, there was continuous archaeological monitoring on site. Archaeological reports on the dune predicted that the likelihood of burials in the top layer of the dune, above a lithified sand cap, was negligible. Our cultural predictions were just the opposite, and these proved to be correct. It is to C. Brewer's great credit that once grading began to uncover burials in the upper levels of the dune, it made a decision to not continue grading to a three-to-one slope but to stabilize the dune as it was in order to prevent the further disturbance of burials.

So now we have at Waiehu a very important piece of what I would call the vestigial landscape, important not only because it is a cemetery for unmarked burials, but also because it is one of the few traces left of a magnificent geological and natural feature of the area.

Finally, we come to the last large, relatively undisturbed sand dune formation on Maui at Waihe'e, where a foreign developer proposes to build a golf course in an area rich with archaeological sites and unique natural features including an undeveloped shoreline, a wetland, a stream, and a magnificent sand dune with an elevation in excess of 300 feet. This is not an example of a vestigial landscape but one that is closer to the original landscape of the place. And it is all the more precious for being so.

Even though there is general acknowledgment that the dune at Waiheʻe contains unmarked historic and prehistoric burials—there are also several marked historic cemeteries on the high dune—the developer still hopes to be able to construct a golf course on portions of the dune, as high as 70 feet in several places and as high as 110 feet in another location to carve out a golf tee. A golf cart path is also proposed for construction across a portion of the makai face of the dune.

Yet to be resolved is the question of whether or not such a development is appropriate or compatible given the use of the dune during both prehistoric and historic periods as a burial place. Would, for instance, a golf cart path be tolerated within the boundaries of any marked historical cemetery? And if not, shouldn't the same standard apply to unmarked prehistoric and historic cemeteries and burial sites?

There is no doubt that the dialogue about historic preservation issues has developed over the past few years so that out of recent conflicts has come a deeper understanding and accord between community, government, and development interests. For Hawaiians, respect for our ancestors can take no more primal a form than the responsibility to protect and preserve their burial places.

Struggle for the Soul of Maui

30

MAUI COUNTY COUNCIL MEETING
DECEMBER 18, 1992

When last we left this issue two weeks ago, on December 4, the council granted first reading approval for the Waiheʻe Project District. At that time Planning and Economic Development (PED) committee chair Vince Bagoyo emphasized that one of the primary reasons for granting the requested approval was that after four years it was time to make a decision. These comments of the planning chair eerily echoed statements made by the developer's attorney, Eric Maehara, at the end of the November 17 public hearing when he declared that it's been "four years of permit processing, four years of archaeological studies," and so on.

The council has a duty to act expeditiously on matters of this nature, but to suggest that the council has been dilatory in this particular instance defies the record of these proceedings. To recap briefly, it's appropriate to note again the earliest dates assayed for this project area to give the time line depicted on this sheet an appropriate context.

The four earliest dates are AD 960, AD 1010 (a date obtained during Dr. David Clark's work at the Waiheʻe midden site), AD 1041, and AD 1042. We are discussing at least a thousand years of habitation in this particular area.

Leaping forward, Sokan, a Japanese corporation, purchased the

property from Wailuku Agribusiness in 1988, which is apparently the underlying date of council member Bagoyo's statements that the project has been awaiting a decision for four years.

On November 20, 1990, the State Land Use Commission approved the redistricting of certain lands within the project area subject to twenty-eight conditions. These conditions were amended in May of 1991 when the developer presented a revised golf course layout plan.

On December 17, 1991, the Planning Commission recommended Phase I approval for the Sokan golf course.

On July 8, 1992, the first meeting of the PED Committee was held on this project district/change in zoning request. At that time, Chair Bagoyo, in response to requests by the Cultural Resources Commission, the Office of Hawaiian Affairs, and others, deferred the subject proposal until the final archaeological reports were submitted and reviewed by appropriate entities—a reasonable and well-substantiated decision on the part of the chair.

opposite
Lilikalā Kameʻeleihiwa and Dana Naone Hall face the ancestors in the Waiheʻe Sand Dune.
Photograph by Masako Cordray.

Fieldwork for Phase II testing had been completed in May of this year, two months prior to the July 8 PED meeting.

The next meeting of the PED Committee took place on October 6 when the archaeological reports were made available to various reviewing agencies. The PED chair announced that agency and departmental comments on the reports be submitted to the PED Committee within two weeks. Bear in mind that the three-month period between the first and second PED Committee meetings was due to the fact that the final archaeological reports had not been completed.

On October 21, the PED Committee asked to schedule a public hearing both to satisfy project district requirements and because the final archaeological reports had not been accepted by DLNR—again, a delay caused by the developer's consultant.

The public hearing was held on November 17.

The archaeological reports were revised and resubmitted, and serious pressure was applied to the gas pedal as this project district approval process sped along, beginning with the November 24 vote by the PED Committee to recommend first reading approval despite the fact that a new golf course layout plan was presented for the first time.

This was followed on December 4 by the council's vote to grant first reading approval and not to recommit this item to committee.

opposite

Dana Naone Hall receiving a crash course in shoreline processes from University of Hawai'i Mānoa geology and geophysics professor Chip Fletcher at the Waihe'e shoreline. The brief tutorial helped in mounting a successful challenge of the golf course developer's shoreline certification application.

Photograph by Masako Cordray.

Two weeks later, here we are posed for second and final reading approval by the council.

It appears that many of the council members are ready to justify second reading approval by claiming that such action supports those members of the Waihe'e community who back the golf course. Remembering, of course, that not all residents of Waihe'e support this project. Nor, as testimony throughout the course of this approval process—and especially the testimony you heard today—has made obvious, members of the larger Hawaiian community on Maui and in the state are opposed to a golf course in these shoreline lands. We're asking this council to take a leadership role.

Letter to Michael Lee, Operations Division Chief, US Army Corps of Engineers, and Claudia Nissely, Western Region Office of Review Director, Advisory Council on Historic Preservation

REGARDING SECTION 404 PERMIT APPLICATION BY WAIHE'E OCEANFRONT HAWAI'I INC. AND SECTION 106 REVIEW OF THE WAIHE'E GOLF CLUB PROJECT
JUNE 21, 1994

Dear Mr. Lee and Ms. Nissely:

This letter is written in further support of Hui Alanui o Mākena's (Hui) request, by letters dated June 10, 1994, to the US Army Corps of Engineers and the Western Region Office of the Advisory Council on Historic Preservation, that the Section 106 process be immediately initiated for the Waihe'e Golf Club Project, and that the Hui be recognized as an "interested person" and allowed to participate as a consulting party.

The Hui is very concerned that certain historic properties located within the project area have not been properly identified and/or evaluated. The identification and evaluation of historic, including cultural, properties within the project area is a necessary first step in the Section 106 process, which then involves assessing the effects of the proposed undertaking on the identified properties and developing alternatives to avoid or reduce adverse effects on these properties.

Based on a review and analysis of the information contained in various reports and plans prepared by Paul H. Rosendahl, PhD, Inc. (PHRI), the consulting archaeologist for the golf course project, the Hui challenges the accuracy of PHRI's identification of a number of sites and features and the significance evaluations and general treatments recommended for these certain sites and features.

The Archaeological Inventory Survey of the project area was conducted in four stages. The initial inventory survey as reported in *Archaeological Inventory Survey, Proposed Waihee Golf Club Project Area* (Donham 1989) resulted in the identification of 88 sites with a minimum of 195 component features. Supplemental inventory testing was then conducted at four sites resulting in the identification of approximately 43 additional features—primarily prehistoric agricultural and habitation features; see *Additional Archaeological Subsurface Testing, Proposed Waihee Golf Club Project Area* (Donham 1992). This was followed by Phases I and II testing for burials.

The Hui's concerns regarding the identification and evaluation of sites and features within the project area center primarily on the results of Phases I and II testing contained in two reports: *Additional Inventory Survey Non-Burial Findings* (Boudreau and Jensen 1992) and *Additional Inventory Survey Burial Findings* (Boudreau and Jensen 1992). Initially, the reports on Phases I and II testing identified 15 "loci" (a term for which there is no known federal or state historic preservation parallel) consisting of approximately 161 subsurface features. When pressed as to the definition and relevance of identifying "loci" in lieu of sites, PHRI revised the reports and asserted, instead, that with the exception of six newly identified burial sites, all of the "loci" could be "linked" to and included with previously identified sites.

The Hui strongly disagrees that the nonburial features of the 15 "loci" are all appropriately linked to previously identified sites, as proposed by PHRI. In some instances, there appears to be little or no archaeological reason for PHRI's linkage of certain Phases I and II features to a particular site. For example, a habitation terrace—Horizontal Feature (HF) 47—and a stacked stone wall—HF 52—are both included in Site 2471, the historic-period Waiheʻe Farm and Dairy Complex. Identified during the initial inventory survey, the farm and dairy complex consisted of 16 farm and dairy structures that Donham declared were "not the logical equivalent of 'features,' as used elsewhere in this report" (Donham 1989, 79).

Unlike the surface structures originally identified by Donham,

HF 47 and HF 52 are subsurface features listed as being of indeterminate age in the Boudreau and Jensen 1992 report. It would appear that if these features are part of a historic site, their age of necessity must also be historic. Data on HFs 47 and 52 in the Boudreau and Jensen 1992 report suggests probable prehistoric age. For instance, indigenous (prehistoric) artifacts as well as significant amounts of midden were recovered from both features.

The PHRI reports uniformly state that one of the principal research goals of the Archaeological Inventory Survey was to "determine the functions and periods of use" for sites and features in the project area. Donham's initial inventory survey satisfactorily achieved this research goal; general functional interpretations were determined for all but 20 (approximately 10%) of the 195 features Donham recorded. Age determinations were made for all except 27 (14%) of the 195 features.

The results of Phases I and II testing fell short of the research goal. No functional interpretation was made for 27 (17%) of the 161 features. In addition, another 13 features (representing 8% of the Phases I and II features) are listed as being "possible" irrigation features. An astonishing 97 of the 161 features (60%) are listed as indeterminate in age; see Boudreau and Jensen 1992, table 1. It is our belief that the extent, integrity, and value, including the cultural value, of the prehistoric sites and features have been obscured by PHRI's inadequate and/or incorrect identifications and evaluations.

For the Hui, the significant archaeological value of the prehistoric sites and features in the proposed project area is exceeded by their immense cultural value. As such, it is imperative that these sites and features also be considered traditional cultural properties. Evidence of the full range of prehistoric activities dating back at least 1,000 years is present in the Waihe'e shoreline lands. Contained within this well-defined area are agricultural sites—including fishponds and taro pond fields (lo'i), portions of a magnificent irrigation system ('auwai), ceremonial sites (heiau, ko'a), extensive burial sites, landing sites, and fishing grounds. As a consulting party, our group can help provide more effective consideration of the historic and traditional cultural properties present in the area and assist the Army Corps of Engineers in meeting its program responsibilities.

We again urge immediate initiation of the Section 106 process. We are especially concerned that any further delay of the 106 process may result in the foreclosure of alternatives to avoid or reduce the adverse effects of the undertaking, which would otherwise be available. We look forward to hearing from you very soon.

Sincerely yours,
Dana Naone Hall

Probable Ceremonial Object 32

COMMENTS SUBMITTED TO STATE HISTORIC PRESERVATION DIVISION ON ARCHAEOLOGICAL FINDINGS AT WAIHE'E, MAUI

MARCH 11, 1993

In table 1, on page 10 of the revised *Non-Burial* report (Boudreau and Jensen 1992), Horizontal Feature (HF) 86 is described as a rock concentration of indeterminate function and age in Excavation Unit (EU) 31. Disturbed prehistoric and historic debris were not collected, according to the notation in the "Associated Remains" column. This information is contradicted by the data contained in table A-1, page A-15, where a glass fragment is recorded in Layer IA of EU 31, while table A-2, on page A-33, shows that an octopus lure and a basalt flake were collected from Layer IA. A basalt flake was also collected in Layer II.

One other indigenous artifact, listed as a modified basalt item of uncertain function, was retrieved from EU 31. Leslie Kuloloio and I happened to see this basalt artifact soon after it was taken out of EU 31. The *Non-Burial* report does not identify this artifact as having come from EU 31, so it would have been nearly impossible to determine its provenience had we not been present at the site shortly after its discovery in the first days of Phase II testing. The description of this artifact on page 58 of the *Non-Burial* report states:

> Two specimens are classified as large waterworn cobbles, and have little or no specific modification to suggest a specialized function.

> The smaller cobble (Acc. 401) has an "X" etched into its surface, suggesting that it could have served as a kuleana or property marker, while the larger of the two stones (Acc. 112), *encountered in association with a platform*, might have been interpreted as a ceremonial object. Lack of any secure context for the specimen prohibits further speculation or interpretation of their possible functions, however. The stones measure 50 by 25 by 18 cm and 40 by 21 by 17 cm respectively. (Emphasis added)

The presence of one glass fragment in a surface layer cannot be used as a pretext to ignore the more compelling presence of prehistoric artifacts of greater number and importance; in particular, an octopus lure* and an upright stone that is probably a ceremonial object on the order of a kūʻula.

The stone recovered mauka of the wetlands (formerly the site of Kapoho fishpond) fits the following description contained in the Pukui and Elbert *Hawaiian Dictionary*:

> **kūʻula.** Any stone god used to attract fish, whether tiny or enormous, carved or natural, named for the god of fishermen; open altar near the sea for worship of fish gods; *but where fish gear was kept with* kūʻula *images so that gear might be impregnated with* kūʻula *mana, usually inland and very taboo. Lit.*, red *Kū*. (Emphasis added)

*An engaging account of cowry-shell lures (comparing the desirable traits of cowries to the attractions of a beautiful woman) appears in Kamakau's *The Works of the People of Old*. The use of cowry-shell lures to catch octopuses was one of "two 'aristocratic' (haʻaheo) ways of fishing that [was] . . . widely engaged in." (Kamakau 1992B, 67)

The spring-fed Waiheʻe wetlands in the early to mid-1990s. I ka wā kahiko, Kapoho fishpond, located in these shoreline lands, contributed to Waiheʻe being an ʻāina momona.
Photograph by Masako Cordray.

On a calm day the sparkling
water at the edge of the cave
is irresistible
if you are alone husband
brother father friend be careful
or the water will appear to
greet you in the form of a woman
you could disappear for days
or even weeks before you
are found again with no memory
of where you have been
gasping like a fish in air

Hāna Golf Course Testimony

34

MAUI COUNTY COUNCIL

SEPTEMBER 17, 1993

Good morning, council members. As with any number of other final decisions rendered by this council in the last nine months, the decision you will make on the Hāna golf course bills later today is not in any doubt. There is always the possibility that the council will not approve the pending bills, but that possibility is remote. About as remote as the possibility that the construction of a golf course will make the hotel profitable—or will itself be profitable.

Although this council may not set much store by what many of us who advocate maintaining Hāna as a Hawaiian place have to say, it's important to speak for the life of the land and not just the economic life that can be wrung out of the land. The representations of outside investors are accepted with little in the way of rigorous examination by this council, while residents of Maui are kept at the periphery of the decision-making process.

This is ironic given the fact that all county legislation, like the Hāna golf course bills, states: "Be it ordained by the people of the County of Maui." If a vote or impartial survey of the people of Maui were to be taken by the council, there is little doubt that the wishes of the people would tip in favor of denying approval for a golf course in Hāna. So these words at the beginning of the Hāna golf course bills are meaningless. The people of Maui do not ordain a golf course in Hāna but the majority of this council does.

The council's inability to assess and heed the will of the people and to truly serve the public interest is underscored by a resolution that will also be considered later today—a resolution to remove Tom Morrow as vice chair of the council and elevate Dennis Nakamura. Tom Morrow's election as vice chair was one of the few signs the public has had that the council had a flickering interest in maintaining at least a semblance of democracy. Today, just as surely as dissenting views in the public are not accorded much weight and respect by the council, we will witness the enactment of this same disregard and disrespect on a dissenting member of this body.

Please do not mollify us with statements about it being the chair's prerogative to choose the vice chair. Why is it so imperative to choose another vice chair nine months later? Is the chair abusing his so-called prerogative? I think so. Is the chair's prerogative more important than the signal it sends to the public that dissenting views are not welcome? Apparently so. What makes the council think that the public would have more confidence in Dennis Nakamura as vice chair? Where was Mr. Nakamura on the public service and community service scene prior to his election last November? Why, on a golf course, of course, as that is his place of employment. So I suppose it all makes a kind of chilling sense.

But lest this council think that this is purely a lament, let me assure you that those of us who do not agree with your actions will not be deflected by your vote today. This golf course is a long way from being constructed. As with so many issues that I have been involved in, when we are told up front that there is no way that we can prevail, we will continue to watch and wait and to assist where we can in maintaining the life of the land forever.

Elliot Cades Award for Literature Introductory Remarks

35

POETRY READING AT HONOLULU ACADEMY OF ARTS
OCTOBER 5, 1990

A few weeks ago I read a newspaper horoscope for my sign, which predicted that Jupiter would be entering one of my houses. The auspices as related by the newspaper column were so favorable that I laughed. But here I am, thanks, in part, I suppose, to Jupiter.

And thanks to the Hawai'i Literary Arts Council for giving me this award on the basis of Tony Quagliano, Joe Stanton, and Anthony Friedson's selection. I can only say that they must have been dazzled by the stars.

I am thankful as well to Charlotte and Russell Cades for establishing the Elliot Cades Award for Literature. I know that there are attorneys in the Cades family, and while I am not an attorney, my husband is, and what I do for a living often involves the legal complexities of the land use process. So this award combines for me, in some measure, the worlds of poetry and law—at least it brings them closer together. And the day itself has combined those worlds. Earlier today, on Maui, I was a member of a panel at an archaeological conference. Where once I used to feel at ease reading poetry, I now feel more at ease delivering a talk on historical and cultural preservation.

I am originally from O'ahu, but for the past fourteen years I have lived on Maui, where I find myself witnessing all over again what I witnessed as a child—the urbanization and suburbanization of what was an essentially rural place. I am still startled by the view of the Honolulu cityscape that's presented as one comes hurtling off the airport interchange. It is disturbing to see so much of the land literally covered over. In any case, I didn't come here to give you one of my political talks—although if you're interested, see me later.

Jacques Cousteau, in advising his son Jean-Michel on the best means of involving people in efforts to save the environment, wisely said, "People will protect what they love." So tonight to a Hawai'i we all love, I offer a few poems.

Hawaiʻi '88

36

FOR LEAHI

The way it is now
few streams still flow
through loʻi kalo
to the sea.
Most of the water
where we live
runs in ditches alongside
the graves of Chinese bones
to the great central valley
where the same crop
has burned in the fields
for the last one hundred years.
On another island,
a friend whose father
was born in a pili grass
hale in Kahakuloa,
bought a house on a concrete
pad in Hawaiʻi Kai.
For two hundred thousand
he got window frames
out of joint and towel racks
hung crooked on the walls.
He's one of the lucky ones.
People are sleeping in cars
or rolled up in mats on beaches,
while the lūʻau show hostess
invites the roomful of visitors
to step back in time to

when gods and goddesses
walked the earth.
I wonder what she's talking about.
All night, Kānehekili
flashed in the sky
and Moanonuikalehua changes
from a beautiful woman
into a lehua tree
at the sound of the pahu.
It's true that the man
who swam with the sharks
and kept them away
from the nets full of fish
by feeding them limu kala
is gone,
but we're still here
like the fragrant white koki'o
blooming on the long branch
like the hairy-leafed nehe
clinging to the dry pu'u
like the moon high over Ha'ikū
lighting the way home.

Looking for Signs

37

Aunty Alice said it first
there had been hōʻailona
ever since we took up
trying to keep the old road
from being closed in Mākena
on the island where Māui
caught the sun in his rope.
The foreign owners of a half-built
hotel don't want their guests
to taste the dust
of our ancestors in the road.
They want them to step
from the bright green clash
of hotel grass to sandy beach
and the moon shining on a rocky coast.
The last hukilau in that place
was ten years ago,
but people still remember
the taste of the fish and the limu
that they gathered on the shore.
When tūtū gets sick
the only thing that brings her back
is the taste of the ocean
in soup made from the small
black eyes of the pipipi.
In her dreams ʻopihi
are growing fat on the rocks.
She is old and small now

Aunty Alice Kuloloio on the Honuaʻula coast ready to exercise her shoreline gathering rights.
Photograph by Dana Naone Hall.

in her bed above the blue ocean
wrapped in the veil of her dream
like the uhu asleep
after a day of grinding coral into sand.
It was at this house on Sunday
that relatives who stayed home from church
saw a cloud of dragonflies appear
over the ocean and fly through the windows.
Higher up the mountain someone else
dreamed of seeing Pele's canoe
on the water the red sail of Honuaʻula
coming toward land.
One weekend the family slept
at another beach along the old road
the old road that is the old trail.
Uncle Charley took us all to the heiau
mauka of the beach.
From the beginning he has said
the road will not be closed.
When we came back,
Ed, one of the boys from Hāna,
was standing in the shallow water
sending the sound of the conch shell
and the winding breath of the nose flute
across the channel to Kahoʻolawe
through the ear of Molokini.
Later, we listened
to Uncle Harry joke with the kūpuna.
Tūtū was there and she stayed
all night sleeping in the sand
with the ʻaumākua all around.
The moʻo clucked in the kiawe,
while pueo flew through the dark
cutting across the path
of the falling stars,

and manō ate all the fish but one
in the net that Leslie laid.
As for us,
what is our connection to Mākena?
You pointed out that we live on
one of three great rifts out of which
lava poured in ages past
to form the mysterious beauty of Haleakalā.
Two gaps press in on the rim of the mountain
like a pitcher with two spouts.
Koʻolau separates us from Hāna
and Kaupō divides Hāna and Mākena
but there is no gap between us
and Mākena lying at the bottom of
the youngest rift, where the
sweet potato vines covered the ground.
This morning, coming back along the coast,
on our side of the island
where the road bends at Hoʻokipa,
I saw a cloud shaped like a pyramid
and a car driving out of the sun.

Ka Moʻolelo o ke Alanui 38

THE STORY OF THE ROAD

More than four hundred years ago,
as it comes down to us,
the road was built by Kihaapiʻilani,
who spread his cape over Maui.
When the ʻōhiʻa blossoms were
tossed by the wind
he travelled to the island of Hawaiʻi
to ask for ʻUmi's help,
and returned with a fleet of canoes
and warriors to conquer Hāna.
From Hāna the rest of the island
fell to him like a ripe fruit.
In the years that followed,
the farmers and fishermen,
native tenants of the land,
placed on the brow of the coast,
as it circled the island,
a road to catch the falling sound
of the runner's feet.
Kūkini carried messages past
petals of cliffs opening in mist.
Near the shore, the akule,
silver black and still quivering,
was divided among
the paddlers and those who helped
bring in the nets.
The white tapa hung from the pole
announced the arrival of Lono Makua

during the Makahiki.
Feathers and the food of the land
were brought to the ahu
along the road where the god
in his pig form was waiting.
Closer to our time, cattle
crossed the road and were herded
to the anchored boat.
Poi, wrapped in ti leaves,
came by way of another boat from Kīhei.
Horses, oxen and wagons stirred up
the dust of the road,
pausing at the one store, where hands
exchanged things over counters,
then continued on into this century.
Now there is car surf on the road
and the waves keep breaking.
Dust mixing with salt air.
After all these years,
we are being told that the road
will be closed. Those who propose it
don't know that the road is alive.
Give up the road they tell us
and it will be replaced
with a sign that says
we can get to the beach this way,
only don't get off the path
or cut across the grass,
and hang on to your children
not to mention don't loose your
cooler until you hit the sand.
For all your troubles
there'll be a comfort station
in the parking lot (a comfort to whom?)
and even a concrete trail

to mark where the old road once passed
between the hotel and the beach,
open so many hours a day
and closed when the sun goes down.
The lizard woman is talking
but who is listening?
At night,
when the island is deep
    in the crater of sleep,
across the channel
  the moʻo
    raises its head
one eye reflecting the moon.

Uncle Eddie Chang Sr. on the makai side of the Mākena Road with the Maui Prince Hotel under construction in the background.
Photograph by Dana Naone Hall.

The Road to Cultural Justice 39

SAA ARCHAEOLOGICAL RECORD,
THE MAGAZINE FOR THE SOCIETY
FOR AMERICAN ARCHAEOLOGY
JANUARY 2013

"Ka Moʻolelo o ke Alanui" (p. 119) expresses an ongoing connection to the old coastal road in the Mākena area, which evolved from the ancient trail that circled the island of Maui. Our work, as Hui Alanui o Mākena, in preserving this important traditional access to the shoreline led us to Honokahua. Culturally and spiritually, we walked on the trail to reach Honokahua where a three-year-long battle to protect the Honokahua Burial Site began.

The trail next led us to Waiheʻe where a five-year struggle occurred over preservation of this wahi pana. The magnificent sand dune at Waiheʻe, nearly 300 feet above mean sea level, appears as a crescent-shaped feature embracing and defining the two shoreline ʻili of Kapoho and Kapokea where at least three heiau were built, and one, Kealakaʻihonua, is still visible today. The Waiheʻe dune was used over a longer period of time even than the dunes at Honokahua, and houses yet more iwi kupuna.

After many years of working on burial issues, it is my belief that if iwi kupuna are protected and left undisturbed in their homeland where they were laid to rest, we too have a home. Burial sites are an integral part of our sovereignty as Hawaiian people. These ancestral burial places constitute sovereign ground.

The work I have engaged in for nearly thirty years, protecting and preserving historic and cultural sites and lands, has rubbed against the political grain. In fact, anyone who knows Maui issues might be tempted to say that I have a problem with authority. But even powerful economic and political forces can be deflected on occasion to save some irreplaceable part of our collective heritage. The desecration of the Honokahua Burial Site was a foregone conclusion before our involvement. Powerless to prevent the excavations, all we could do was insist on agreements made as to the manner in which the digging would occur. In this Theresa Donham, the project field supervisor, assisted us. She adhered meticulously to the agreements and was always forthcoming, truthful, and informative about the excavations. She also made it clear that she thought the excavation was wrong. I learned a great deal about archaeology, practiced at a high level at Honokahua (albeit in service to an unjust end), which caused me to examine the ethical and moral dimensions of the profession. Many Hawaiian oli and moʻolelo speak of companions on the way. In this respect I would like to acknowledge my husband, Isaac Hall, my companion dissident. And since I spoke briefly about Waiheʻe, I would also like to acknowledge Burt Sakata, who was one of the Waiheʻe community members instrumental in saving those precious coastal lands from golf course development. In the heat of the controversy, very few contemplated a different fate for Waiheʻe.

I am astonished by the elements of our past that still exist—many of which archaeological activities uncover. I deliberately refrain from referring to what is found as fragments because doing so suggests that we are fragmented ourselves. To me, gratitude is an appropriate response to encountering and being in touch (literally) with still-existent sites.

For example, on the island of Oʻahu, intact, traditional burials were found beneath urban fill in the original matrix of a backshore dune system mauka of Ala Moana Boulevard. I now see that area with different eyes. In another instance, if one stood on the second floor balcony of ʻIolani Palace a hundred years ago and looked west, beyond the ancient burials continuing their moe loa at Kawaiahaʻo, the shoreline of Honuakaha would be visible just makai of Queen Street.

The ancient pathways to ancestral sites continue to be traveled by our imaginative and spiritual selves. A spark of kinship can bridge centuries of time in the flash of a moment, as occurred to me one day at Waiheʻe when I unexpectedly saw the top half of a lei ʻōpuʻu (a bud-shaped neck ornament) and realized I was the first Hawaiian to see this ornament since it had been separated from the person to whom it belonged.

Because of an abiding interest in continuity and the possibilities of reconnection, I do not relish being the last person, or among the last, to glimpse a site before it is destroyed, especially before we have an understanding of what that site may be—its age, function, significance, and part, if any, in a larger pattern. There is often an essential conflict with developer-driven archaeology, which attempts to navigate the regulatory process as quickly and inexpensively as possible. The desired outcome is that historic preservation review will have as little effect as possible on land development plans.

Unfortunately, far too many historic sites given State Inventory of Historic Places (SIHP) numbers end up being destroyed because they are considered significant for Criterion D (information content) only, and are neatly and irrevocably written off by the declaration that sufficient information has been obtained from the site. I have come to think of Criterion D as the default criterion. An ironic tragedy is that many of the sites consigned to destruction by the liberal use of this criterion are precontact or early historic in age and thus of particular value to Hawaiians. Yet, the purported information obtained from sites so designated rarely reaches beyond a handful of individuals.

Hawaiʻi's historic preservation laws place an affirmative duty on the state and its political subdivisions, the counties, to protect and conserve historic and cultural sites for future generations. The historic preservation review process in Hawaiʻi relies on Archaeological Inventory Surveys (AIS) and the reports those surveys generate.

Since most surveys are conducted in a land development context, these situations are ripe for conflict. The necessity for an adequate survey is illustrated by an example from Maui of an extensive historic and cultural complex that is in danger of being destroyed before we know what is present and can make wise decisions about what should be preserved.

The area of concern is an open midland above the town of Kula with the distinctive octagonal-sided Holy Ghost Church in the lower right-hand corner (figure 1, p. 128). A sinuous line of green, which marks Keāhuaiwi Gulch, bisects the 272-acre parcel, slated for subdivision development. Literally translated, Keāhuaiwi is the bone shrine or the bone altar. Despite its evocative name, the majority of the gulch located within the project area has not undergone an AIS.

The curve of a graded access road can be seen on the south side (to the right) of the gulch as well as numerous terraces, walls, and rock mounds. A multitude of surface features are also present on the north side. In all, 1,349 archaeological features were identified. The great majority of those features (1,218), located on both the south and north sides of the gulch, were incorporated into one SIHP site number, Site 50-50-11-6338. Lumping together an unprecedented number of features from different temporal periods into one vast noncontiguous site spread over several hundred acres raises serious concerns. The following bullet points further question the accuracy and adequacy of the inventory survey report.

- The AIS report does not include a large-format map that clearly shows the locations and feature numbers of the 1,349 features recorded. The tiny 5½-by-8-inch map that is provided depicts features as minuscule squiggles, dots, and lines, none of which are numbered.
- Only three out of 743 terraces were subjected to subsurface testing. None of the terraces associated with Site 6338 were tested.
- The second most numerous category of features was rock mounds. None of the 309 rock mounds were tested, with the result that their functions and ages are listed as unknown. Rock mounds marking or sheltering burials have been found elsewhere in Kula and are present in other moku on Maui as well. It is well known that burials are an integral component of the settlement landscape. Not testing features where burials are likely to be found frustrates the purpose of an AIS.

- Twenty-five features out of 1,349 (less than 2%) were tested. Many of these test units were only 0.5 by 0.5 meters in size. Test units were terminated due to "time constraints" even when subsurface architecture was found. Provisional language appears throughout the AIS report. Examples include the interpretation of a terrace as "a possible precontact habitation feature," the presence of "possible uprights," and "possible" pieces of unidentified bone noted at other features.
- Out of 1,349 features, only sixty-eight features are designated for permanent preservation.

Thirty-nine sites were newly identified, according to the AIS. The only sites slated for preservation on the south side of Keāhuaiwi Gulch were two small enclosures, one of which is shown in figure 2 (p. 129). Both enclosures are single-feature sites assessed as significant for Criterion D only, and therefore are being preserved on an interim basis as "data banks." No testing was conducted on either enclosure during the AIS, and their ages are listed as undetermined. Long terrace walls, as well as numerous rock mounds, surround the enclosures.

On the northern side of Keāhuaiwi Gulch, there are excellent examples of historic ranching features. None are earmarked for preservation (figures 3 and 4, pp. 130–31). The AIS acknowledges that the parcel contains one of the few remaining upper elevation (2,972 to 3,107 feet) agricultural field systems, including the remains of an extensive ʻauwai system. Given the great number of agricultural and habitation features indicating long periods of successful farming activities and settlement, it is inconceivable that heiau and other structures devoted to ceremonial purposes were not identified during the AIS. Religion was at the heart of precontact society in Hawaiʻi, and places where offerings were made to the gods and ceremonies conducted to ensure fertility and productivity would have been an inextricable part of the cultural landscape.

As the name Keāhuaiwi indicates, this land is a quintessential kulāiwi. A supplemental AIS that addresses the numerous, serious inadequacies of the current report is not only warranted—it is a matter of cultural justice (Naone Hall 2013).

Fig. 1. An aerial view of a relatively intact historic complex above the town of Kula on the island of Maui.
Photograph by Masako Cordray.

Fig. 2. One of two single-feature enclosure sites slated for interim preservation. The orange tape marks a 5-meter buffer around the site.
Photograph by Masako Cordray.

Fig. 3. Historic ranching features on the north side of the gulch.
Photograph by Masako Cordray.

Fig. 4. A closer view of some of the ranching features.
Photograph by Masako Cordray.

Grand Wailea Proposed Renovation and Guest Room Expansion Project

40

TESTIMONY BEFORE THE
MAUI PLANNING COMMISSION
OCTOBER 13, 2009

Note: This testimony was provided to the Maui Planning Commission in the hope that the details would restore some human dignity and presence to the burials and offer a glimpse of the deep life of the place.

Good morning, commissioners. An Archaeological Inventory Survey (AIS), according to the Hawai‘i Administrative Rules, Section 13-276-3, shall

> determine if archaeological historic properties are present in the project area and, if so, identify all such historic properties.

In the Grand Wailea case, the AIS will be performed *after* the Special Management Area permit is granted, when there will be much more pressure to relocate burial sites if they are found in inconvenient locations for the permitted development.

This is not the way an AIS should be performed. The information about historic properties, and cultural and historic sites, must be available to decision-makers prior to the granting of a permit, in particular before the last discretionary permit for development in the coastal zone. A monitoring plan is no substitute for an AIS. Let's review briefly the history of the Grand Wailea site with respect to archaeological issues.

In 1986 Paul H. Rosendahl, PhD, Inc. (PHRI) conducted an AIS of the project area, which resulted in the identification of two sites of particular interest. Site 2012 was a rectangular walled enclosure located on an elevated knoll in the northeast corner of the parcel near the area later designated for the reinterment of burials from Sites 2802 to 2804. This site was dated AD 1620 to 1890. The enclosure was interpreted as ceremonial in nature.

Site 2013 included two raised stone platforms, which marked two burials. This site complex included hearths and other subsurface features and was used prehistorically as a habitation site from approximately AD 1340 to 1600. A thousand artifacts were recovered during the inventory survey, indicating intensive habitation of this area.

In 1987 monitoring commenced for construction of the Grand Wailea hotel. This was approximately the same period of time during which excavation of the Honokahua Burial Site began. The difference is that the Hawaiian community and the public at large did not know about the extensive disturbance of burial sites at the Grand Wailea. Neither PHRI (the project archaeologist), nor the hotel developer (TSA International), the State Historic Preservation Division, or the Office of Hawaiian Affairs informed the general public and Native Hawaiians of the potential effects of this project on Native Hawaiian burial sites.

The result of this monitoring project was the identification and relocation of a minimum of 344 individuals, including the disinterment of 119 primary, in situ burials. Among the individuals identified were the human skeletal remains of burials unearthed in the 1970s during the construction of a county sewage pump station and associated pipelines.

These burials were unearthed a second time during the 1987 to 1990 monitoring program.

Isn't it time we show some respect to the iwi kupuna that remain in their place of interment, their resting place and home?

Monitoring resulted in the identification of three additional burial sites within the project area. Sixty-three artifacts directly associated with human skeletal remains were recovered. Fifty-nine of these artifacts were found in association with burials located at Site 2802 where 79 burials were recovered, the majority of which were primary burials.

It should be noted that almost all of the burials were disturbed by mechanical excavation, either bulldozer or backhoe. It may sometimes seem abstract to talk about burial sites and their disturbance, so I will attempt to give you a sense of the individuality of some of these burials.

For instance, Burial 5 was found in a seated position. The burial pit in which this adult male was buried was filled with eleven layers of large rocks and midden. Interlaced with the large rocks immediately above the burial were small smooth stones (ʻili ʻili). This burial was found at a depth of almost 3 meters or 10 feet deep.

Or Burial 9, where the remains of an infant were severely impacted by a backhoe. This severe damage to the remains of infants was the case throughout the project area. The skeletal remains of small children are very fragile and often disintegrate when contacted by machinery—no matter how controlled the monitoring.

A number of burials were found covered with white or black fibrous material—kapa. Burial 25 was a female found in a seated position on a layer of ʻili ʻili, her body wrapped in black tapa.

Burials were found with fish placed a few centimeters away from their mouths. Burial 46, an older adult male, was found facing west with his arms crossed on his chest and a lei niho palaoa placed in the neck region.

Site 2803 consisted of 28 primary burials and 13 clusters of previously reinterred remains. The monitoring plan notes that during the excavation of the main sewer drain, the remains of 5 individuals were disturbed by heavy equipment. These 5 individuals were buried at depths between 4 and 6 meters, or 13 to nearly 20 feet below the surface.

In another instance, excavation for the Luau Building disturbed four burials. All were found in sand and were severely impacted by construction activity.

Site 2804 parallels the coastline extending for a distance of over

65 feet. Twelve individuals were excavated from the sand at Site 2804. The remains of a four- or five-year-old child disturbed by grading activities was found buried with a dog, which was placed to the west of the body of the child. Site 2804 was used for burial purposes contemporaneously with habitation.

Wailuku Sand Dune Burials

41

TESTIMONY PREPARED FOR MAUI/LĀNAʻI ISLAND BURIAL COUNCIL MEETING
SEPTEMBER 26, 2012

I am disheartened to learn that two more burials were found during the removal of fourteen burials at the VMX site in Wailuku adjoining the Kihei Gardens property. To say that many of us were correct in predicting the high likelihood that additional burials would be found is small comfort. There may be even more burials in this remnant dune.

A little background—by letter dated December 1, 2009, the original fourteen inadvertent burials were determined, after careful analysis by State Historic Preservation Division (SHPD), for preservation in place. SHPD noted that the burials were located in an area with a concentration of skeletal remains and that Hawaiʻi Revised Statues Section (HRS §) 6E-43 and the administrative rules dictated greater consideration for preservation in place. Furthermore, the geographical, regional representative for the burial council concurred that the burials should be preserved in place. It wasn't until January 23, 2012, nearly two years and two months later, that the Department of Land and Natural Resources, through William Aila, the State Historic Preservation Officer, issued a letter revising the determination to preserve in place and, instead, approving relocation. Neither the regional representative nor the Maui/Lānaʻi Island Burial Council were informed ahead of time of this about-face determination.

I raise this issue because I do not see anything in the rules that allows for reconsideration of a determination after such a lengthy period of time. For instance, an applicant unhappy with a burial council determination has forty-five days following receipt of written notification of a council determination to file an appeal of the determination and request a contested case. See Hawaiʻi Administrative Rules Section (HAR §)13-300-51.

For the inadvertent discovery of human remains, in accordance with HAR §13-300-40, the department shall determine preservation in place or relocation following the application of criteria that include the requirement to give greater consideration for preservation in place to burials located in areas with a concentration of skeletal remains. The rules also require consultation with appropriate council members. Within ninety days following a determination to preserve in place or relocate, the department shall approve a burial site component of either a preservation plan or an archaeological data recovery plan.

The September 14, 2012, letter of determination for newly discovered Features 26 and 27 of Site 6060 does not contain any mention of consultation with the burial council's geographical representative and the results of that consultation. When decisions are allowed to be made without the participation of all interested and affected parties, the process becomes susceptible to manipulation and distortion. We all have to abide by the same rules.

I won't speculate about how or why this situation occurred. What I am interested in is a restored process that is open and fair to all participants and offers the protections afforded by law to our ancestral burials.

The Disappearance of the Traditional Hawaiian Landscape in Kakaʻako/Kewalo 42

O'AHU ISLAND BURIAL COUNCIL MEETING
SEPTEMBER 8, 2010

Note: This case represents a failure on the part of both the State Historic Preservation Division (SHPD) and the Oʻahu Island Burial Council to properly treat and protect significant sites in the Kakaʻako and Kewalo area.

On September 13, 2006, the Oʻahu Island Burial Council voted 6–4, with then-chair Jace McQuivey participating in the vote, to relocate eleven previously identified burials found in two general locations of the 5-acre Victoria Ward Village Shops project area. General Growth Properties (GGP) requested relocation and insisted that it could not change its development plans and that all of the burials were beneath the footprint of buildings.

Yet in 2004, GGP sought and received approval from the Hawaiʻi Community Development Authority (HCDA) for modification of the initial approval of its base zone development provisions, authorization for the execution of a joint development agreement and approval for a development permit for the project. The proposal increased the buildings' maximum height limitation from 45 feet to 220 feet. The project as modified would encroach into the view corridor setbacks on Kamakeʻe and Queen Streets and encroach into the front yard along Auahi Street.

I mention the HCDA approvals for two reasons. First, the Archaeological Inventory Survey (AIS) for the Victoria Ward Village Shops project should have been done as part of GGP's application to HCDA. AISs are comparable to Environmental Impact Statements. They identify important resources that require protection early in the approval process, when the widest range of planning options is available. If the AIS had been done at this early date, the ability to preserve in place the burials encountered in the project area would have been greatly increased.

This brings me to my second point. Perhaps this council would consider writing a letter to HCDA to recommend that an AIS be required for any projects under HCDA's jurisdiction prior to the issuance of development permits to afford maximum flexibility in accommodating the preservation of significant historic sites.

One of the oddities of GGP's project was that inventory testing began in some areas while building demolition occurred in other areas under a SHPD-approved monitoring plan. Well before the inventory survey report was completed and the AIS report submitted to SHPD, GGP was allowed to monitor ground disturbance activities concurrently with inventory survey investigations. The first burial was encountered on February 10, 2006; SHPD received the AIS report by Cultural Surveys Hawai'i more than three months later on May 24, 2006, and accepted it twelve days later on July 5, 2006. The speed of SHPD's review is mind-boggling.

The AIS identified three historic sites: a historic fishpond, which is also referred to as a prehistoric fishpond (Site 6856); a traditional cultural layer and five burials not associated with the cultural layer (indicating that the burials were older than or predated the cultural layer) in the Waikīkī end of the property (Site 6854); and a traditional cultural layer with six contemporaneous burials in the project's 'Ewa end (Site 6855). The AIS calls Site 6855's cultural deposit "rare" and "unique," claiming that no other archaeological investigations in the Kaka'ako area "have documented a similar traditional Native Hawaiian subsurface cultural deposit." Further, the AIS found, and SHPD concurred, that this cultural layer "has integrity of location and materials" and is therefore significant for Criterion C, as an excellent example of site type. Site 6855's cultural layer is also significant for its information content, Criterion D, and for Criterion E, due to the presence of associated burials.

It is interesting that for the numerous determinations made regarding the eleven previously identified burial sites and the fifty-four inadvertent burial discoveries, none of the determinations noted that any of the burials were found in areas within a context of historic properties—one of the primary criteria for giving greater consideration for preservation in place. Another primary criterion for greater consideration of preservation in place is, of course, burials located within a concentration of human skeletal remains. The criteria for whether to preserve in place or relocate are the same whether the island burial council or SHPD makes the determination.

Burial Sites and Preservation Areas Located within the Keōkea Farm Lots Subdivision

LETTER TO DEPARTMENT OF HAWAIIAN HOME LANDS
CHAIR RAYNARD SOON
NOVEMBER 27, 2002

Dear Chairperson Soon:
This letter is written on behalf of the Maui/Lāna'i Island Burial Council. At a regularly scheduled meeting on October 31, 2002, the burial council voted unanimously to authorize its vice chair to send a letter that sets forth for your consideration the council's comments and recommendations, at this time, on burial sites and preservation areas in the Department of Hawaiian Home Land's Keōkea Farm Lots Subdivision.

BACKGROUND

An archaeological inventory survey was conducted for the Keōkea and Waiohuli Subdivisions, the results of which are contained in a November 1989 Archaeological Inventory Survey Report (AIS) prepared by Paul H. Rosendahl, PhD, Inc. The inventory survey report identified 108 historic sites on 351 acres in Keōkea and 51 historic sites on 674 acres in Waiohuli. These figures indicate that more than twice as many sites were found in Keōkea as in Waiohuli, on approximately half the amount of land.

During the AIS, seven burial and/or probable burial sites were identified: Site 2028, Site 2029, Site 2089, Site 2084, Site 2097, Site 2311, and Site 2339.

Subsequent to the inventory survey, archaeological data recovery was conducted earlier this year by Scientific Consultant Services Inc. on 20 out of 39 permanent habitation sites. Four more burial sites were discovered in the course of data recovery work: Site 2049, Site 2050, Site 2032, and Site 2034.

POTENTIAL THAT OTHER BURIAL SITES ARE PRESENT WITHIN THE PROJECT

Significantly, burials were found at 20 percent of the habitation sites that underwent data recovery. This percentage indicates a relatively high occurrence of burials in the Keōkea habitation sites. The burial council has the following comments.

- Generally, only one excavation unit (1-by-1 meter) was excavated in each feature of the 20 historic sites selected for data recovery. In this context, it is all the more remarkable that burials were encountered at four different sites. For example, during the excavation of a 1-by-1-meter unit inside a large enclosure approximately 130 square meters in size at Site 2034, an in situ burial was found just below the surface.
- The great majority of burials were encountered at shallow depths (within 35 centimeters or approximately 1 foot of the surface).
- In addition to the four burials discovered during data recovery, other burials may be present at one or more of the 20 habitation sites that underwent data recovery.
- There is a high likelihood that burials may also be present at one or more of the 19 habitation sites that did not undergo data recovery.
- The project area is covered with dense vegetation that may conceal burial sites that have not yet been identified.

CONCERNS ABOUT THE ACCURATE LOCATION OF SITES

The burial council is concerned that the location of the historic sites shown on map plans by SSFM International Inc. may not be accurate, primarily due to the fact that the sites have not been surveyed. As an example, the location of Site 2089 is shown on Drawing No. C-1, dated June 2002, as a crosshatched area mauka of Road "A." However, field observations of Site 2089 indicate that the site is located partly within the Road "A" corridor. Similar inaccuracies are likely for other sites as well.

Site 2089 is slated for preservation in place. If a portion of Site 2089 and/or its preservation buffer area are within the roadway corridor, this conflict should be addressed before final plans are approved.

RECOMMENDATIONS

The burial council offers the following recommendations to the Department of Hawaiian Home Lands.

- Prior to the construction of roadways within the project area, including grading or grubbing activities, the council recommends that the roadway corridor be surveyed and staked and an archaeological consultant be given the opportunity to conduct a walk-through reconnaissance of the corridor. The reconnaissance will confirm whether or not any historic sites are within the roadway corridor.

- If any sites are found during the roadway reconnaissance, archaeological testing should take place prior to a determination of appropriate treatment for the site.

- An archaeological monitor should be present during construction of the roadways and other infrastructure.

- If inadvertent burials are encountered, the council recommends that preservation in place be considered as the first option.

- Finally, the burial council recommends that the main original archaeological preserve, shown as a crosshatched area within bold black lines, on Exhibit "A" attached to this letter, be expanded to encompass the areas outlined in yellow. The area to the south, in particular, contains a significant concentration of sites.

Most of the area proposed for expansion of the preserve appears to lie almost entirely within Phase II. The burial council welcomes the opportunity to consult further with the department on the location of a roadway for Phase II along the southern end of the preservation area. Greater flexibility may also be afforded by the fact that the Keōkea Farm Lots project is part of a Department of Hawaiian Home Lands tract that is more than 6,000 acres in size.

The expanded preserve area will encompass 14 of the 20 sites selected for data recovery: Site 2046, Site 2047, Site 2048, Site 2030, Site 2050, Site 2059, Site 2061, Site 2032, Site 2072, Site 2073, Site 2074, Site 2081, Site 2082, and Site 2034. (The majority of these permanent habitation sites are located along a ridgeline, which is a significant part of the cultural landscape that will be preserved by designation of the larger area.) In addition, at least six of the eleven known burial sites will be protected within the larger preserve.

The burial council greatly appreciates the opportunity to consult with you and the department on this important matter.

Sincerely,
Dana Naone Hall
Vice Chair

The Brescia Case 44

LETTER TO STATE HISTORIC PRESERVATION OFFICERS AND ADMINISTRATOR Regarding *Archaeological Inventory Survey of a 15,677-Square-Foot Parcel in Wainiha Ahupua'a, Halele'a District, Island of Kaua'i, Hawai'i*, and *Preservation Component of a Burial Treatment Plan for Multiple Burials Discovered on an 18,106-Square-Foot Parcel*

JUNE 16, 2009

Dear Laura Thielen, Pua Aiu, and Nancy McMahon:

This letter concerns the Archaeological Inventory Survey (AIS) and the Burial Treatment Plan (BTP) prepared by Scientific Consultant Services Inc. (SCS) for Joseph Brescia. Both documents contain errors, contradictory statements and missing information, among other deficits, and must be revised to comport with Hawai'i Administrative Rules Sections (HAR §§) 13-276-1 et. seq. and HAR §§13-300-1 et. seq., respectively, as well as HAR §§13-284-1 et. seq., Chapter 284, titled "Rules Governing Procedures for Historic Preservation Review to Comment on Section 6E-42 Projects."

I submit the comments that follow, as an interested person, concerned about the adverse effects of the proposed residential project on a significant historic and cultural property.

I. Archaeological Inventory Survey for the Brescia Lot

In December 2007, SCS concluded the second phase of archaeological testing on Lot 6, within the Wainiha subdivision. A draft AIS on the results of the survey work was submitted to the State Historic Preservation Division (SHPD) sometime in January 2008. By SHPD letter dated January 24, 2008 (Log No. 2007.4124/Doc No: 0801NM06), Nancy McMahon determined the report "acceptable."

The SHPD's acceptance letter consists of fewer than 200 words, less than a page. Although the letter mentions that radiocarbon dates for State Site 50-30-02-1878 (cultural deposits and human burials) range from AD 1150 to 1820 (mid-twelfth to early nineteenth centuries), SHPD concurs that Site 1878 is significant under Criteria D and E only.

It should be noted that although these comments are being submitted nearly a year and a half after SHPD received the AIS for this property, compliance with HAR §13-284-3 states in pertinent part:

> (f) The SHPD shall afford interested persons an opportunity to comment on submittals' acceptability in accordance with this and related rules. . . . *Comments must be submitted in writing to the SHPD within thirty days of the SHPD's posting a notice* of "no historic properties affected" determinations or posting a notice of SHPD receipt of documentation. The SHPD shall post notice every Friday of receipt of relevant documents and of issuance of SHPD "no historic properties affected" or receipt of information. The notice shall be posted either at the SHPD office or on the SHPD's website. (Emphasis added)

Notice of the receipt and availability of this AIS was not posted at the SHPD office or on the SHPD's website, denying interested persons the opportunity to comment on the document. In any event, Nancy McMahon's acceptance letter written for the SHPD was clearly issued less than thirty days after receipt of the document.

No consultation with potentially interested organizations and individuals occurred as a result of this lack of notice. Thus, the views of interested parties "on the identification, significance evaluations, and mitigation treatment" of Site 1878 were not considered "in a good faith and appropriate manner during the review process" (HAR §13-284-2). I first learned of the AIS for this project when I reviewed the May 27, 2009, BTP (Draft 11) on May 30, 2009 (the AIS is referred to in the BTP). I obtained a copy of the AIS on June 2 and began my review of the document two days before the meeting of the Kauaʻi/Niʻihau Island Burial Council (KNIBC) on June 4, 2009. This letter is written within thirteen days (nine working days) of receiving the AIS.

A. Identification of Project Parcel Survey Area/Area of Effect

The cover page of SCS's AIS identifies TMK (4) 5-8-009:045 as a 15,667-square-foot parcel. However, the introduction, on page 1 of the report, describes the parcel as "an approximately 18,000-square-foot lot" owned by J. Brescia. The BTP similarly identifies Parcel 45 as 15,667 square feet in size. A review of Kauaʻi County tax records indicates that this parcel is 0.4157 acres or 18,106 square feet. HAR §13-276-5(a)(1)(B) requires identification of the survey area "in the text, stating . . . the acreage of the parcel." Identifying the correct size of the parcel is important for a number of reasons, including the accurate calculation of the areal extent of the property covered by the inventory survey.

For instance, if only a tenth of the parcel was tested during the inventory survey (a generous assessment of the amount of testing conducted in this case) and thirty burial features were found (this does not take into account the minimum number of individuals identified, which is a higher number), then extrapolating from this data places the approximate number of burials on the parcel at three hundred. Whatever the actual number of burials may prove to be, the extensive presence of human burials on this parcel is likely to result in numerous encounters with "inadvertent burial discoveries" during construction. Since the AIS testing was completed, there have been one or two more burials identified, including a burial encountered during the installation of a dust fence (the latter as related to the KNIBC by Nancy McMahon at its June 4, 2009, meeting). *The area of effect involves the entire parcel, not just the proposed residential footprint*. HAR §13-276-2 defines project area as "the area the proposed project may potentially affect, either directly or indirectly."

B. Presence of a Traditional Cultural Property/ Necessity for an Ethnographic Survey

A traditional cultural property is defined in HAR §13-284-2 as:

> any historic property associated with the traditional practices and beliefs of an ethnic community or members of that community for more than fifty years. These traditions shall be founded in an ethnic community's history and contribute to maintaining the ethnic community's cultural identity. Traditional associations are those demonstrating a continuity of practice or belief until present or those documented in historical source materials, or both.

When a traditional culture property is identified, according to HAR §13-284-5(b)(5)(B):

> *An ethnographic survey may be undertaken when the SHPD concludes that* traditional cultural properties are present or likely to be present within the project area and when *the project area is known to have been used by members of an ethnic community at least fifty years ago or by preceding generations*. (Emphasis added)

Nancy McMahon, writing for the SHPD, acknowledges in her January 24, 2008, letter that the radiocarbon dates for the Site 1878 cultural deposits are AD 1150 to AD 1820, establishing continuous use of the project area by Native Hawaiians for many generations and triggering the necessity for an ethnographic survey.

The AIS itself notes on page 6:

> The parcel's proximity to the rich resources of Wainiha Bay and the fringing reef of Lae o Kaonohi are ideal locations for a full range of fishing activities of all kinds, from reef collecting to offshore pelagic operations. *Because of this rich resource Wainiha has most likely been the site of Hawaiian settlement as long as people have inhabited the island of Kauai*. (Emphasis added)

The parcel is located "approximately one-half mile northwest of the Wainiha River." Water is described as plentiful in Wainiha, where "numerous streams run across the land," feeding into the Wainiha River (AIS, p. 6).

The availability of surface water and sand dunes in a hospitable windward environment made this area of Wainiha a favored place for Hawaiian settlement for at least seven or eight centuries. The cultural deposits, including copious midden, and the presence of ancestral burials at the Brescia parcel, certainly fit the definition of a traditional cultural property worthy of an ethnographic study.

This position is underscored by the fact that the SHPD is aware, at least through Nancy McMahon, that the connection of present-day Native Hawaiians to the particular area at issue is strong, vital, and continuous. Numerous Native Hawaiians have written and testified about the responsibility to protect and preserve the burials, and the inappropriateness of building a portion of the proposed residence over some of the burials.

Furthermore, Mr. Jeffery Chandler, a Native Hawaiian who worked, until recently, for more than ten years for the DLNR/SHPD as the caretaker of the Ahu o Laka at nearby Kēʻē in Hāʻena, grew up on the sands of Naue, fishing and shoreline gathering like many generations of his ancestors before him. He and others with direct knowledge of the area should have been included early on in the historic preservation review process.

C. Significance Evaluations/Site 1878 Is Significant under Criteria A, B, D, and E

Site 1878 possesses integrity of location, setting, feeling, and association. SCS has evaluated this site as significant for criteria D and E. However, based on information contained in the AIS and other sources, Site 1878 is significant under criteria A and B as well.

(1) CRITERION "A." BE ASSOCIATED WITH EVENTS THAT HAVE MADE AN IMPORTANT CONTRIBUTION TO THE BROAD PATTERNS OF OUR HISTORY.

The settlement pattern in the project area is present in the multiple cultural layers and deposits, which evidence the centuries-long permanent habitation of the Wainiha shoreline and backshore.

The "Traditional and Historic Setting" section of the AIS relies principally on Handy and Handy's *Native Planters in Old Hawaii*. At one point, the authors of the AIS selectively edit a quote from J. M. Lydgate, which appears in *Native Planters* (1972, 419), as follows:

> We have an interesting description of the population of Wainiha in the early 19th century before whites had come in (Lydgate 1913, 125–127).
>
>> At a time as late as the reign of Kaumualii, the local konohiki making a careful census of the valley by villages from the sea mauka returned upward of 2,000 souls. Enumerating in detail all the communities, he gave the exact quota from each—*Naue*, Pa-ie-ie, Maunaloa, Pali-eleele, Maunahina, Pohakuloa, Opaikea, Homai-ka-lani and ending with Laau, the hamlet farthest mauka in the depths of the mountains, where the valley contracts to a narrow gorge, with a brawling stream running white in the bottom. . . . All along up the river, wherever the encroaching palis on either side leave the least available space, the land has been terraced and walled up to make "lois." And so the whole valley is a slowly ascending stairway of steps, broad in the tread and low in the rise, all the way to Laau, where the last available space was won, if not by the dwarfs, at least by someone who understood this kind of agricultural engineering. (Emphasis added)

Incredibly, the AIS uses a portion of the same passage from Lydgate, but omits the reference to Naue. The truncated version appears on page 8 of the AIS:

> and so the whole valley is a slowly ascending stairway of steps, broad in tread and low in the rise, all the way to Laau, where the last available space was won. (Lydgate 1913, 125–127)

Ample historical documentation exists, confirmed by archaeological investigations, of the long period of precontact settlement, which extended into the postcontact era, within the project area. The living descendants of the iwi kupuna at rest in the one hānau of Naue continue their efforts to protect the sanctity of this significant site.

Finally, HAR §13-284-6(c) states that:

Prior to the submission of significance evaluations . . . the agency shall consult with ethnic organizations or members of the ethnic group for whom some of the historic properties may have cultural significance under criterion "e" *to seek their views on the significance evaluations*. For native Hawaiian traditional cultural properties *the Office of Hawaiian Affairs also shall be consulted*. (Emphasis added)

HAR §13-284-6(d)(1)(c) further requires:

> Evidence of any consultation shall be submitted with the [significance] assessment, to include:
> (i) A description of the consultation process used;
> (ii) A list of the individuals or organizations contacted; and
> (iii) A summary of the views and concerns expressed.

Unfortunately, the AIS prepared by SCS, and accepted by the SHPD for Parcel 45, contains no evidence of any consultation, in violation of this section of the rules governing evaluations of significance.

(2) CRITERION "B." BE ASSOCIATED WITH THE LIVES OF PERSONS IMPORTANT IN OUR PAST.

In the section of the AIS titled "The Mahele and Beyond" (9–10), the following statements appear:

> Wainiha Ahupua'a was retained by Miriam Kekau'onohi, granddaughter of Kamehameha I and wife of Ke'ali'ihonua [*sic*], the son of Kaumuali'i, Chief of Kaua'i. (Barrère 1994, 327)*
>
> Royal Patent No. 7194 was acquired by Mikahela Kekauonohi and included Wainiha Ahupua'a in Halele'a. An LCA [Land Commission Award] was presented to M. Kekauonohi as LCA: 11216:2 at Wainiha. . . . (Waihona 'Aina 1998). Mikahela Kekauonohi was the granddaughter of Kamehameha I and wife of Liholiho Kamehameha II, Keli'iahonui [*sic*], and Ha'alelea. Because M. Kekauonohi did not have children, there were no immediate heirs to her holdings. (Waihona 'Aina 1998)

*The information on page 327 of Dorothy Barrère's *The King's Mahele: The Awardees and Their Lands* includes the listing of the Wainiha, Halele'a, Kaua'i land award to Kekau'onohi but not the biographical information included in the AIS by SCS.

Appendix A: LCA Data in the AIS contains scant information on Kekau'onohi's ties to the 'Āina at Wainiha.

In *Native Land and Foreign Desires: Pehea Lā E Pono Ai?* Lilikalā Kame'eleihiwa states that of the ten Ali'i Nui in the *Buke Māhele*, Kekau'ōnohi controlled the fourth largest amount of land prior to the Māhele. After the Māhele, Mikahela Kekau'ōnohi, following payment of the government commutation fee, possessed the second largest number of 'Āina, with only the King, Kauikeaouli, exceeding her holdings. When she died in 1851 (she was forty-six), her extensive 'Āina were left to her second husband, Levi Ha'alelea (Kame'eleihiwa 1992, 307).

Significantly, in deciding which 'Āina to keep (mālama) and which 'Āina to relinquish (of 129 'Āina, 52 were relinquished and 77 held), Kekau'onohi chose to retain the 'Āina at Wainiha—one of only six lands that she held on Kaua'i (Kame'eleihiwa 1992, 243). As Dr. Kame'eleihiwa makes clear:

> In the *Buke Māhele*, the *'Āina* were enumerated in the Hawaiian way—by individual place names. Hawaiians had an intimate knowledge of and a poetic attachment to the *'Āina*, naming each valley, ridge, stream, hill, and even rocks with special metaphoric terms. Each name had a story or distinct personality. Previously, and for hundreds of years, each inventory of *'Āina* was remembered without the aid of written records. *The 'Āina was part of one's family*. (Ibid, 232; emphasis added)

In addition to being an Ali'i Nui and direct descendant of Kamehameha I, Mikahela Kekau'ōnohi was the Kia'āina (Governor) of Kaua'i for eight years, from 1836 to 1844. As the Governor of Kaua'i, she also was a member of the Privy Council, along with the Governors of the islands of O'ahu, Maui, and Hawai'i, and five ministers. She was the only female Governor and the only woman on the Privy Council. Surely her association with the 'Aina at Wainiha, which includes the project area, is sufficient to declare Site 1878 significant under Criterion B.

D. HAR §13-284-7 Determining effects to significant historic properties

This provision recognizes that effects "include direct as well as indirect impacts" and further elucidates that:

> (b) Effects include, but are not limited to, partial or total destruction or alteration of the historic property, *detrimental alteration of the properties' surrounding environment, detrimental* visual, *spatial*, noise, *or atmospheric impingement. . . . These effects are potentially harmful.* (Emphasis added)

Effect determinations are to be submitted to SHPD for review, along with "the survey report, significance assessments and mitigation commitments" (HAR §13-284-7(c)).

Although the burials encountered during backhoe trenching of the project area are the subject of a separate BTP, the language in this section of the rules aptly applies to the burials. Building a portion of the proposed house over some of the burials would certainly result in the detrimental alteration of the surrounding environment for those particular Site 1878 burials, imposing detrimental spatial and atmospheric impingements, as many Native Hawaiian cultural practitioners, scholars, and organizations have stated loudly and clearly.

E. HAR §13-284-8 Mitigation

Once again, the rules recognize that:

> If properties with cultural significance, so evaluated under criterion "e" as defined in §13-284-6(b)(5) are involved, the agency shall initiate a consultation process with ethnic organizations or members of the ethnic group for whom the historic properties have cultural significance under criterion "e" to seek their views on the proposed form of mitigation. For native Hawaiian traditional cultural properties the Office of Hawaiian Affairs also shall be consulted.

Consultation on significance evaluations, determining effects, and mitigating the effects to historic properties with cultural significance can be consolidated and take place at the same time, so long as the consultation occurs before the SHPD's acceptance of the inventory survey. It is highly likely that consultation with interested persons and the Office of Hawaiian Affairs (OHA) for Site 1878 (cultural deposits and burials) would result in the rejection of SCS's recommendation of data recovery as an appropriate form of mitigation. Consultation is an important missing component that must take place.

On page 112 of the AIS:

> SCS opines that any human burials that will be impacted by the Phase IIc foundation layout, and the other human burials found during Archaeological Monitoring on this parcel, should be Data Recovered, with profile and plan view drawings, if sufficient data on them has not been previously collected.

This opinion of SCS shows no respect for Site 1878.

F. General Comments

- The section on background research, here called "Traditional and Historic Setting," is deficient and must be revised to conform to HAR §13-276-5(b).
- There is no clear statement about the extent of survey coverage and no careful and meaningful discussion of the sampling design as required by HAR §13-276-5(c)(3). For example, what percentage of the parcel was sampled?
- With the exception of the burial features, most if not all of which the backhoe disturbed either directly or indirectly (by subsequent trench wall collapse), there is little discussion of the integrity of the other subsurface features (post holes, pits, hearths, and so on), as required by HAR §13-276-5(d)(G).
- A section on midden analysis should be included in the AIS, especially as the predominant land use pattern of the project area, for centuries, was permanent habitation with access to and use of abundant marine resources.

- A section discussing the features identified during the inventory survey, and their functions, including a table detailing the number of features found and categorizing them by function, is needed.
- Why was there no change in the testing methodology from backhoe trenching to hand-excavated units once burials began to be found, as is the usual and preferred protocol, especially in the immediate area of any burial discovery? Backhoe trenching also resulted in the loss of provenience information for virtually every artifact collected during the inventory survey, an unfortunate circumstance that should have been addressed and avoided.
- At least one significant artifact listed in Appendix B: Artifact Analysis, as a quartz-like pendant fragment, a lei ʻōpuʻu, was found in the back dirt of ST-4. This artifact is not mentioned in the discussion of ST-4 or anywhere in the main body of the AIS.
- The burial depths listed in table 2, for every burial, are different from the depths reported in the "Results" section of the AIS. What are the correct depths?
- Figures 5 to 9 are too small, not to scale, and confusingly labeled; several figures are practically illegible.
- It is essential that a large map, to scale, showing the locations of all the burials (Phase I and Phase II) and human skeletal remains (for instance, the left occipital fragment) be included in the AIS.
- There is no consistency among the plan views. Some are well done and informative; others are poorly executed or labeled beyond recognition.
- A map showing the location of the LCA awarded to Mikahela Kekauʻōnohi should be included in the AIS, pursuant to HAR §13-276-5(b)(C)(ii).
- Consultation with individuals knowledgeable about the project area's history should be conducted, and consultation with interested persons, including Native Hawaiian individuals and organizations such as the Office of Hawaiian Affairs, must be conducted on significance assessments, effect determinations, and mitigation treatments (HAR §13-276-5(g)(1)(A-D).

G. Reconsideration of Findings after the Process Is Closed

According to HAR §13-284-11:

> (a) The SHPD shall reconsider the findings under §§13-284-5 (adequate identification/inventory procedures), 13-284-6 (significance evaluations), 13-284-7 (determination of effects), and 13-284-8 (mitigation), when new information is submitted by an interested party with a request for reconsideration.

Please consider the foregoing comments a request for reconsideration by the SHPD. I incorporate by reference in this request for reconsideration the further comments on the AIS made in Section II of this letter. I am looking forward to receiving SHPD's written conclusions within ten (10) working days of the date of this letter.

II. Preservation Component of a Burial Treatment Plan for Multiple Burials Discovered on a 15,677-Square-Foot Parcel Prepared for Joseph Brescia

As noted earlier, the identification of the size of the Brescia parcel in the BTP is incorrect. It is a 0.4157-acre or 18,106-square-foot lot. This less than one-half-acre parcel contains a *concentration* of burials, yet, the BTP and the AIS before it do not describe the numerous burial features as a concentration. HAR §13-300-2 defines "Areas with a concentration of skeletal remains" [as] "any location where multiple human skeletons are present."

Identifying the Brescia lot as an area containing a concentration of human skeletal remains is very important given the following provision of the Rules of Practice and Procedure Relating to Burial Sites and Human Remains:

> §13-300-1 Purpose
> ... The legislature finds that Native Hawaiian burial sites are especially vulnerable and often not afforded the protection of law, which assures dignity and freedom from unnecessary disturbance (e.g., Honokahua). In order to avoid future disputes arising from the discovery of human skeletal remains fifty years or older, sections 6E-11, 6E-12, 6E-43, 6E-43.5, 6E-43.6, HRS, were amended or enacted in

> part *to provide additional protection for Native Hawaiian burial sites of high preservation value such as areas with a concentration of skeletal remains*, or prehistoric or historic burials associated with important individuals or events, that are within a context of historic properties, or have known lineal descendants. (Emphasis added)

Our Hawai'i burial law, the underlying authority, begins by stating, in no uncertain terms, "All burial sites are significant" and proceeds to recognize in Hawai'i Revised Statutes Section (HRS §) 6E-43(b) that:

> *burial sites of high preservation value, such as areas with a concentration of skeletal remains*, or prehistoric or historic burials associated with important individuals and events, or areas that are within a context of historic properties, or have known lineal descendants, *shall receive greater consideration for preservation in place*. (Emphasis added)

The unequivocal, plain language of the burial statute and the rules make it clear that areas of concentrated skeletal remains shall receive "greater consideration" for preservation in place. My purpose in writing this letter is to help assure the integrity and implementation of HRS §6E-43 and the administrative rules promulgated thereunder.

I was deeply involved with efforts to prevent the archaeological excavation of the Honokahua Burial Site on Maui—from challenging the issuance of a Special Management Area permit to the landowner in 1986, to the ultimate cessation of the digging in December 1988. I participated in the restoration of the disinterred iwi back to their resting place and supported the passage of HRS §6E-43 in 1990. I served as a member of the interim Maui/Lāna'i Island Burial Council (MLIBC) to advise the DLNR-SHPD on burial matters prior to the establishment of the formal councils under §6E-43. I was a member of the MLIBC, serving as the vice chair and chair, at different times, for a total of sixteen years. I have been an active participant in burial and repatriation matters for the past twenty-two years.

It is my belief that a great number of Native Hawaiian burial sites have been protected from unnecessary disturbance, whether direct or indirect, as a result of the harsh lesson of Honokahua and the subsequent passage of Act 306, which added HRS §6E-43 to our state's historic preservation law. The BTP, prepared by SCS for Joseph Brescia, with its proposal to "preserve" six of the thirty burials (20% of the burials) by capping these burials with concrete, then building a portion of the residence over them, is a perverse distortion of both §6E-43 and the administrative rules implementing the burial law. Moreover, the magnitude of this proposal for previously identified burials is without precedent. In fact, approving this BTP would set a very dangerous precedent that could lead to the demise of the burial law and the protections it affords the iwi kupuna.

A. The Preservation Component of the Burial Treatment Plan Relies upon the Adequacy of the Archaeological Inventory Survey

HAR §13-300-24 states that:

> (a) The primary responsibility of the council shall be to determine preservation or relocation of previously identified Native Hawaiian burials, as set forth in this chapter.

The role of the department is to provide the councils with "all necessary support services" including, according to HRS §13-300-28(4):

> Acquir[ing] and verify[ing] all information necessary for a council determination of burial treatment and refer[ing] the matter to the council for determination.

Under HAR §13-300-33, titled "Request for council determination to preserve or relocate native hawaiian burial sites," the department "shall assure that the burial treatment plan includes the following information prior to any council determination."

> (10) Any project plans requested by the council including, but not limited to, construction and grading plans;
>
> (11) A copy of the Archaeological Inventory Survey Report where requested by the council.

At its meeting on June 4, the KNIBC expressed concerns about the construction of a septic system and the potential for encountering additional burials. Michael Dega of SCS and Nancy McMahon showed the council a map depicting the general location of the system, and Michael Dega claimed that the entire area for the septic system had been tested with negative results. I questioned him about whether testing had covered 100 percent of the septic system area, and he said yes. Based on the backhoe trench locations in the AIS, it does not appear that Michael Dega is correct.

The backhoe trenches are referred to as Stratigraphic Trenches (ST) in the AIS. Figure 5, on page 17 of the AIS, is a smaller version of the map Michael Dega and Nancy McMahon displayed to the KNIBC. This map depicts ST-29. The description of ST-29, on page 98, is as follows:

> Trench ST-29 was placed to test the proposed location of a leach field, and to locate subsurface archaeological deposits (Figures 80 and 81). Six layers were exposed during the excavation of the unit [a description of the first five soil layers follows.] . . . The sixth layer in the unit was composed of dry, very pale brown sand interspersed with beach marine shell and beach coral. One basalt octopus lure was found in the trench backfill.

Figure 80 is a photograph of the east wall profile of ST-29 and figure 81 is a stratigraphic profile of ST-29's east wall. Neither figure provides much additional information.

Unlike the text for most of the other trenches, the descriptive text for ST-29 does not offer any trench dimensions. However, table 2 on page 28 provides the information that the trench was 41.5 meters (about 136 feet) long and 90 centimeters (a little less than a foot) deep. ST-29 was the longest trench excavated, by far, with a width of 36 inches—the width of the backhoe bucket. Judging from its depiction in figure 5, it is a long, narrow trench. It is difficult to believe that an entire septic system can be built in such limited confines.

The actual plans for the septic system, as well as the actual construction and grading plans for the proposed project, should be provided to the council so that the council can assess the true extent of subsurface disturbance likely to occur. For example, where will construction/grading excavations exceed 1 meter or approximately

3 feet in depth? The majority of the previously identified burials were first encountered within 1 meter of the current ground surface.

Beside the BTP, the most important document is the AIS. The AIS is the foundation of the BTP, thus the adequacy of the BTP depends upon the adequacy of the AIS. During my tenures as chair and vice chair of the MLIBC, our council routinely required the applicant's archaeologist to provide a copy of the relevant AIS. I often reviewed the AIS with particular attention to the adequacy of the testing program for burial site identification purposes, and for consistency between the AIS and the BTP. Where relevant, the MLIBC often reviewed construction and grading plans as well.

As a reminder, an important role of the department is to "acquire and verify all information necessary for a council determination." Neither the AIS nor the BTP is adequate or acceptable. Nancy McMahon and History and Culture branch chief Phyllis Cayan did not render the necessary administrative support services to the KNIBC (HAR §13-300-28(a)), nor did they acquire and verify the information necessary for the KNIBC's determination and subsequent deliberations on Draft 11 of the BTP. Contrary to Nancy McMahon's statement in SHPD's January 24, 2008, letter accepting the AIS, the "trench summaries are" *not* "fine."

For example, the depth for Burial 1 (B-1) in the BTP is given as 105 cmbs (p. 13), in table 3 of the plan (p. 9) it is listed at 1.0 meter, while the AIS states "the trench did yield an in situ human burial" at 105 cmbs (p. 26). Table 3 of the same report lists the burial's depth at 1.0 meter (p. 22).

Portions of B-1 "recovered during screening of back dirt" (AIS, p. 26) included pieces of a pelvis and a left radius, phalanges, left femur, and cranium fragments. The in situ part of the burial that was not disturbed and displaced by the backhoe included portions of the cranium, pelvis, and ribs. There is very little information provided for this individual in the AIS or the BTP. Of interest, however, is a quartz-like pendant fragment, probably the upper half of a lei ʻōpuʻu, which was found in the back dirt of ST-4.

This significant artifact is listed in Appendix B: Artifact Analysis as having been recovered from ST-4 backfill (a photo of the artifact can be found on p. B20). Although its provenience was destroyed by the backhoe, it is possible that this rare ornament is a grave good, moepū, associated with B-1. This supposition is supported by table 2, titled "Summary of Trench Dimensions, Positions and Findings" for Phase II investigations, which lists the cultural materials observed for ST-4 as basalt flakes and a hammerstone, and SSFE-9 fire pit/imu. (Note: There are two ST-4s, one trenched in Phase I when B-1 was found and one excavated in Phase II when no burial was encountered.)

Three other artifacts labeled "personal adornments" were found during Phase II investigations, only one of which had any provenience information. Burial 11 and Burial 12 were discovered in ST-13. "Ten percent" of B-11 "was disturbed by the backhoe during unit excavation" (AIS, p. 37; BTP, p. 29). Found on the upper chest area of this 3–12-year-old subadult were Conus and Ni'ihau shell beads. Skeletal elements of B-12 uncovered by the backhoe included a pelvis, a long bone, and "a cranium buried in a pit dug into beach sand" (AIS, p. 60). The AIS states that collapsing trench walls limited mechanical excavations.

Finding two burials (perhaps one with grave goods) in one trench should have dictated a change in methodology to hand-excavated units in the immediate area around these burials to ascertain the presence or absence of additional burials in the vicinity. To underscore this necessity, figure 38, on page 54 of the AIS, which is a Plan View of ST-13, depicts SSFE-17 as a pit location visible in the east wall of the trench. This pit was not investigated, and thus the function of this feature was not determined—another example of the inadequacy of this inventory survey. SSFE-17 may be a burial pit.

A perforated personal ornament made of coral is identified in Appendix B of the AIS as originating in ST-8. However, this information does not appear in the main text of the AIS or in the BTP at all. ST-8 contained two burials—Burials 6 and 7. B-7 was uncovered on June 14, 2007, one of the only burials for which the date of its discovery is provided. Listing the dates for the thirty burials is important for several reasons, including determining how soon the DLNR-SHPD and the KNIBC were notified, and how close in time these finds occurred.

Again, the multiple nature of the finds during relatively limited periods of time, specifically for Phase II a–c when twenty-seven burials were identified in June and July of 2007, should have required a change in methodology to hand-excavated units in areas adjacent to identified burials to determine whether the burial was part of a cluster of burials within, as we now know, a larger concentration in the project area. The AIS contains no rationale for SCS persisting in backhoe trenching after the first burial was identified.

This point is reemphasized by the fact that B-6 is described as consisting of scattered human remains extending from ST-8 into ST-9. The remains in ST-8 were "inventoried as rib fragments, the vertebral body and a phalange" found in Layer II "in a circular depression" (AIS, p. 47). The remains in ST-9 purported to be part of B-6 "were deemed too fragile to excavate . . . they consisted of teeth, cranium fragments and ribs" (ibid.). One wonders what, if any, oversight was being exercised by the SHPD over this project.

The coral personal adornment collected from ST-8 likely was associated with either B-6 or B-7. Neither the AIS nor the BTP discusses the artifacts that were found or their proposed disposition. Other artifacts, collected from the back dirt of trenches that also contained burials, may have been grave goods disassociated from the individuals they were buried with by the backhoe. These artifacts include, but are not limited to, fishhooks, octopus lures, and tools.

Figure 94, which appears in Appendix B, page B20, is a photograph of ten sea urchin spines, graduated in size, with a grooved circular band at one end—these spines were part of a personal adornment. This artifact and three Conus shells (each with a perforation, possibly for a puka shell necklace, as noted in the report on page B5) were found in ST-14. This artifact information is not included in the AIS or BTP's discussions of the findings concerning ST-14.

Burial 13 and Burial 15 were identified in ST-14. ST-14 was a very short trench, only 3.03 meters (about 10 feet) long (see table 2).

Obviously, these burials were found in very close proximity to one another. The artifacts recovered from the trench back dirt were probably associated with one or both individuals. B-13 was determined to be an individual 0 to 3 years of age and B-15 was a 21- to 35-year-old individual. Some of the shortest trenches contained multiple burial finds.

B-6 and B-7, discussed earlier, were found in ST-8, which was 2.9 meters (less than 10 feet) long. Other examples include ST-17, which was 5 meters (approximately 16 feet) long and contained Burial 18 and Burial 19; ST-19 was 4 meters (13 feet) long and contained Burial 21 and Burial 22; ST-21 was 6.8 meters (22 feet) long and contained Burials 24, 25 and 28; and ST-22 was 4.1 meters (13 feet) long and contained Burials 26 and 27. Many of these burials were found in sand pits. If SCS had been hand-excavating 1-by-1 or 1-by-2 meter units many of these burials would have been identified before any adverse effects were visited upon them. The differently colored sand of a burial pit is often an early warning that a burial may be present when excavations by hand are performed and the archaeologist is digging carefully down toward the burial. More than anything, this archaeological project is a story of lost opportunities.

It is ironic that SCS, with SHPD's concurrence, identifies Site 1878 as significant under Criterion D (has the potential to yield information important in prehistory or history) when it conducted archaeological investigations (mechanical trenching) in a manner that resulted in adverse effects on a sensitive site—every burial feature was unnecessarily disturbed, and provenience information for the numerous artifacts encountered—some of which were probably grave goods—was lost. Adding to this irony, SCS recommends data recovery for any burials found during monitoring for construction (AIS, p. 112). SHPD's acceptance letter of January 24, 2008, written by Nancy McMahon, states:

> We concur with your recommendation that archaeological monitoring should take place during construction due to *the high probability of finding additional burials*. An archaeological monitoring plan will

> need to be submitted to our office for review and approval. (Emphasis added)

If the Native Hawaiian community had been aware of this uncivilized—bordering on barbarous—method (backhoe trenching) used to identify burials within the project area, the outcry against such desecration would have been even more insistent.

The information contained in both the AIS and the BTP is incomplete, in part, because the inventory survey did not adequately cover the project area. For instance, the shoreline setback area received no subsurface testing presumably because no construction is allowed in the area. However, burials in the setback area are still at risk if the landowner plans to landscape in this area. Even relatively shallow excavations for landscaping purposes have the potential for disturbing burials.

Naupaka, a shrub often planted on shoreline properties, is well known for its deep, tenacious root system, posing another potential threat to burials. The use of naupaka to demarcate burial locations outside of the residential footprint is an inappropriate measure. Furthermore, naupaka, when it is irrigated as it will be here, is invasive horizontally (covering ground surface quickly) and vertically (deep roots). Concrete caps over the burials are not a deterrent, since the naupaka root system can readily spread beneath the caps.

The legal notice published on April 24, 25, and 29, 2007, in the *Garden Island* newspaper, a copy of which is attached as Appendix B to the BTP, was defective. At the time of publication, the inventory survey had not been completed and only the first of thirty burials had been identified. The notice is full of errors: the Royal Patent number is 7194, not 7165; Mikahela Kekauʻōnohi's first name is misspelled (Makahela); Chapter 6E, Revised Statutes Section 43.5, is cited followed by the statement that "the final disposition shall be made by the SHPD–Burial Sites Program in consultation with KNIBC." As even SCS concedes, this burial and the twenty-nine others are all previously identified burials subject to the jurisdiction of the KNIBC. Lastly, the copy of the legal notice has been reduced in size to the point where a magnifying glass must be used to read it.

SCS's attempt to point to a couple of Maui cases to justify its proposal to "preserve in place" some of the burials, by capping them with concrete and building a portion of the proposed house over them, is dishonest and wholly inappropriate. The only instance that I know of where a house was constructed over burials was an inadvertent discovery and not previously identified burials. As such, SHPD made the final determination. The Waiheʻe example cited by SCS involved a burial preserved in place (kept intact in the sand dune) behind a retaining wall for a house. I cannot respond to SCS's third example involving an unnamed Lahaina project because there is insufficient information to know what is being referred to. None of the Maui projects referred to are identified by the applicant's name or identified by TMK number. The archaeological reports, burial treatment plans, or other archaeological documentation for these so-called precedent-setting projects are not included in the references section of the BTP.

B. General Comments

- An addendum inventory survey should be conducted to include the shoreline setback area.
- Proper legal notice should be published for all the burial features identified in Site 1878.
- The dates for each burial discovery should be included in the BTP.
- Information on the minimum number of individuals (MNI) identified during the inventory survey should be included in the BTP.
- A map, to scale, showing the locations of Burials 1 through 30 and other human skeletal remains identified during the inventory survey should be included in the BTP.
- All pits not examined during the inventory survey, and assigned an indeterminate function, shall be considered possible burial pits.
- Correct the HAR §13-300-40(j) citation (which governs inadvertent discoveries) on page 1 of the BTP to HAR §13-300-33.

- Provisions for the disposition of the artifacts and a discussion of those that may be grave goods should be included in the BTP.

SCS should be directed to develop a Burial Treatment Plan that comports with HRS 6E-43 and §13-300-33 of the Administrative Rules. I incorporate by reference in this section any comments made on the Burial Treatment Plan in Section I of this letter.

Kindly provide all the members of the KNIBC with copies of this letter well in advance of the council's next meeting. Thank you for your anticipated cooperation.

Sincerely,
Dana Naone Hall

Kawaiaha'o Church Multi-Purpose Center 45

HONOLULU AHUPUA'A, KONA DISTRICT, ISLAND OF O'AHU
Letter to State Historic Preservation Officer and Chair of the Board of the Land and Natural Resources Laura Thielen; State Historic Preservation Division Administrator Pua Aiu; Director of the State Department of Health Dr. Chiyome Fukino; Department of Health Registrar Alvin Onaka; Chairperson of the O'ahu Island Burial Council Kawika Mckeague; and Department of Planning and Permitting Director David Tanoue
JULY 2, 2009

I write this letter as an "interested person" because I am a descendant of family members buried at Kawaiaha'o and I am concerned with the effect of the proposed Kawaiaha'o Church Multi-Purpose Center (MPC) project on historic properties, especially burials (HAR §13-284-1(c)(2)). I formally request reconsideration of the determinations contained in Laura Thielen's letter dated June 11, 2009, based upon HAR §13-284-11, and that Ms. Thielen communicate the conclusions of the State Historic Preservation Division (SHPD) of the Department of Land and Natural Resources (DLNR) on the matters set forth below within ten working days from the date of this letter or by July 16, 2009.

Section I of this letter is addressed to Ms. Thielen. Section II is addressed to the DLNR and the State Department of Health (DOH). Section III of this letter is addressed to all of those agencies or entities issuing permits or approvals for the proposed Kawaiaha'o Church Multi-Purpose Center project without an Environmental Assessment (EA).

I. DLNR Must Reconsider

A. Introduction

The burials at Kawaiaha'o are previously identified burials. The burials affected by the project are not located within any "known, maintained, actively used cemetery." Kawaiaha'o Church has been a designated National Historic Landmark for forty-seven years. All National Historic Landmarks are listed in the National Register of Historic Places. Only 3 percent of the places on the National Register are National Historic Landmarks. Kawaiaha'o also is located within the Hawai'i Capital Historic District, which is listed in the National Register such that an EA, at least, must be prepared before any further permits or approvals may be issued for this project and before this project may be implemented any further, based upon Hawai'i Revised Statutes Section (HRS §) 343-5(a)(4).

Your erroneous findings deny Native Hawaiians the hard-won procedural and substantive rights conferred by the legislature in enacting the burial law in 1990. Before 1990, Native Hawaiians were disinterred based only upon the issuance of permits by the DOH, pursuant to HRS §338-25.5. In 1990, the issuance of permits by DOH was deemed legally insufficient to protect the rights of Native Hawaiians and to preserve Native Hawaiian burials and Native Hawaiian burial sites. Your conclusions represent an effort to return to the legally insufficient manner of disinterring Native Hawaiians in force before 1990, and rejected thereafter.

In addition, your illegal determinations constitute a concerted effort by the DLNR, entered in cooperation with the representatives of Kawaiaha'o Church, to circumvent the plain requirements of our state's burial law, which you are charged with upholding. This is an effort to strip the island burial councils of their primary jurisdiction and authority to make decisions about whether Native Hawaiian burials must be preserved in place or relocated, after following procedures and applying substantive standards established by state law and duly promulgated administrative rules. The DLNR does this by issuing erroneous determinations that the burials are "inadvertent discoveries" when the overwhelming available evidence demonstrates that they are "previously identified" burials, thereby placing the burials within the jurisdiction, in this case, of the Oʻahu Island Burial Council.

B. Necessity to Be Clear about Burial Sites and Cemeteries on the Kawaiahaʻo Property

I am not aware of any plot plan for the Kawaiahaʻo property that clearly shows the location of the different burial sites and cemeteries, particularly as these have different legal statuses.

At the request of Kawaiahaʻo Church, or its agent, Cultural Surveys Hawaiʻi Inc. (CSH) prepared, in April 2005, a report titled *Background Information in Support of Subsurface Testing, Monitoring, and Burial Treatment Plans for the Kawaiahaʻo Church Ancillary Facility Project, Honolulu Ahupuaʻa, Kawaiahaʻo ʻIli, Kona District, Island of Oʻahu* (O'Hare 2005). The CSH report was presented to the DLNR and you were aware of its contents when you made your determinations.

The CSH report contains written testimony constituting the previous identification of Native Hawaiian burials, outside of any area that could possibly be construed as dedicated to cemetery use on the Kawaiahaʻo property.

According to the CSH report, there were apparently two cemetery areas on the Kawaiahaʻo Church property, one for the relations of the missionaries and one for church members, primarily Native Hawaiians. There is also the tomb of William Lunalilo, the first elected king of Hawaiʻi. It is located near the corner of King and Punchbowl Streets at the main entrance to the church property.

The Mission Cemetery is located at the rear of Kawaiahaʻo Church. It was first consecrated in 1823. Some of the early missionaries and their descendants are interred at the Mission Cemetery. The Mission Cemetery is not affected by this project.

The 1912 and 1920 Cemetery Maps evidence the use of some of the Kawaiahaʻo property as a cemetery for church members, primarily Native Hawaiians, during a distinct period of time.

The Kawaiahaʻo Church property was a burial site for Native Hawaiians during lengthy precontact and postcontact periods of time, quite apart from the period of time the church may have subjected the property to its burial plot plans. Based upon current evidence, these precontact and postcontact Native Hawaiian burials exist throughout the church property and even within the areas covered by the 1912 and 1920 Cemetery Maps, excepting the Mission Cemetery.

In April 2005, the CSH report alerted Kawaiahaʻo Church and the DLNR that it was possible that some disturbed human skeletal remains or in situ burials remained in the area of the proposed Kawaiahaʻo Church Multi-Purpose Center project. The CSH report therefore recommended the preparation of an Archaeological Inventory Survey (AIS) and subsurface test excavations before commencing construction so that the presence or absence of human burials could be determined.

Kawaiahaʻo Church and the DLNR ignored this recommendation and the written testimony constituting the likely presence of Native Hawaiian burials outside of any areas marked on the surface for cemetery use. As such, in 2009, Kawaiahaʻo and its agents needlessly disturbed, by mechanical excavation, sixty-nine burials on Kawaiahaʻo Church property, outside of the burial plots and marked cemetery areas.

C. History of Repeated Disinterment of Native Hawaiian Burials Should Not Continue on a Standardless Basis

Cemeteries represent that those buried within their boundaries will rest in peace, undisturbed, in perpetuity. This representation does not apply to Native Hawaiians buried at Kawaiahaʻo Church who, history shows, have been disturbed, excavated, and relocated on many occasions between 1838 and the present. The known history of the disinterment of Native Hawaiians at or by Kawaiahaʻo is recited below. It should be noted that Laura Fish Judd commented on April 2, 1828, in her diary on the third of four churches that preceded the current stone church at Kawaiahaʻo: "The church is surrounded by a burying-ground already thickly tenanted" (O'Hare 2005, 24).

1. 1838: Disinterments for Construction of the Fifth Church. During the digging of the basement for the current stone church at Kawaiahaʻo, Native Hawaiian burials of at least six church members, "and perhaps some others," were disinterred and relocated. As Levi Chamberlain related in his diary on July 31, 1838: "In accomplishing this [excavation of the basement] they were obliged to disturb the repose of the dead" (O'Hare 2005, 29).

2. 1916: Disinterments at Waikīkī Branch Church. Kawaiahaʻo sold the cemetery land around its branch church in Waikīkī in 1916 to real estate developers. Thirty-nine individuals, originally buried between 1880 and 1907, were disinterred and relocated. The bodies were to be reinterred in the Kawaiahaʻo and Kamōʻiliʻili Cemeteries. The CSH report notes, "it is possible all of the Waikīkī burials were reinterred in a common grave at Kawaiahaʻo Church in 1916" (O'Hare 2005, 41).

3. 1940: Disinterments for Construction of Likeke Hall. When Likeke Hall was first built, it was constructed on top of a portion of the members' cemetery, identified as Section B, containing 16 burial lots (Lots 15–30). A total of 117 individuals, mainly Native Hawaiians, were disinterred, and the vast majority, including all unknown burials, were relocated to Kamōʻiliʻili Cemetery where they were buried in a common grave to make way for the construction of Likeke Hall. Some of the individuals whose graves were disturbed were Haʻalelea family members, the descendants of aliʻi.

4. 1968: Disinterments When Kamōʻiliʻili Church Sells Its Cemetery. Kamōʻiliʻili Church sold its cemetery for the construction of a new high-rise apartment building in 1968. Of the 466 disinterred burials, the names of only 206 individuals were known. Graves of those reburied in a common grave at Kamōʻiliʻili Cemetery were disinterred again, cremated, placed in small containers, and interred in a vault in the Kawaiahaʻo Cemetery.

5. 1986–1988: Queen Street and South Street/Quinn Lane Disinterments State Sites 50-80-14-4534 and -4532. A total of 116 individuals were disinterred, mostly from a strip of what had been Kawaiahaʻo property, for a road-widening project. The CSH report observes that the burials found during the Queen Street excavations "were located inside what appeared to be old fence posts defining the original cemetery" (O'Hare 2005, 35). The Queen Street remains (Site 4534) were interred "into a vault on the present-day Cemetery grounds" (ibid.).

The CSH report further discusses the Queen Street burial finds on page 35. The report states that 90.5% of the burials were coffin interments and most appeared to be of Native Hawaiian ancestry. Among these postcontact burials, "*one may be precontact and not interred within the old cemetery boundary*" (ibid.; emphasis added). This precontact burial was not assigned a separate site number.

On the same page, CSH reports two apparent Hawaiian practices associated with the burials. Salt was packed in the intestinal cavities of a number of burials, and a number of box burials contained only the skull of an individual. The report then notes: "Both practices appear to be Hawaiian in origin and may be associated with the bringing of ancestral remain [*sic*] to the cemetery after a Hawaiian person had been converted to Christianity." It is not clear who the Hawaiian person is referred to in the foregoing statement—perhaps not the deceased, but a converted family member bringing another family member for burial or reburial in everlasting peace in a Christian cemetery. The older the burials, in other words, the closer in time to early postcontact dates in the eighteenth century, the more likely certain Hawaiian burial practices were still adhered to, including respect for the ancient prohibition against disturbing the dead.

Of further interest are the grave goods found with the burials. Although a large number were Western-introduced, some were clearly early postcontact. For example, coins found dated from 1797 to 1891, placing many of the burials squarely within the eighteenth century. In addition, traditional grave goods also were found, including water-rounded manuports, quartzite cores and a lei niho palaoa, among others (O'Hare 2005, 36).

Finally, the CSH report reveals; "The presence of *several possible prehistoric burials outside the old cemetery fenceline . . . indicates that there may be more burials in the area*" (ibid.; emphasis added).

6. 1986–1988: Punchbowl Street Disinterment State Site 50-80-14-4532. The CSH report does not provide any details on this "isolated" burial.

7. 1986–1988: Halekauwila Street Disinterment State Site 50-80-14-4533. The CSH report does not provide any details on this "isolated" burial.

8. 2002: King Street Disinterment State Site 50-80-14-6371. During archaeological monitoring by CSH, a "*precontact human burial was recovered* near the intersection of King and Punchbowl Streets, *in the area of King Street adjacent to Kawaiahaʻo Church*" (O'Hare 2005, 37; emphasis added.)

9. 2006: CSH Inventory Survey Testing Locates 24 Burials. At the request of Kawaiahaʻo Church, CSH conducted limited inventory survey subsurface testing on Kawaiahaʻo Church property in 2006 and documented the results in *An Archaeological Subsurface Investigation at Kawaiahaʻo Church Cemetery, Honolulu Ahupuaʻa, Kona District, Island of Oʻahu TMK: (1) 2-1-032:016 and 017* (Tulchin and Hammatt 2006). A total of 24 burials were located on Kawaiahaʻo Church property during this very limited archaeological inventory investigation. Only two shallow, narrow backhoe trenches were dug (an average of 55 cm deep in Trench 1 and 40 cm deep in Trench 2, augmented by shovel tests in some areas to 85 cm and 92 cm deep, respectively). The test probes were all less than 1 foot in depth. These burials, by law, are "previously identified" and have never been reported to the Oʻahu Island Burial Council.

10. 2009: Infrastructure for Multi-Purpose Building. In early 2009, Kawaiahaʻo and its agents disinterred 69 burials on Kawaiahaʻo Church property, outside of the burial plots and marked cemetery areas, while constructing infrastructure for the new Multi-Purpose Center at Kawaiahaʻo.

Disinterment and relocation of the Native Hawaiians buried on church or former church property has been a repeated practice by Kawaiahaʻo for almost two hundred years. This is a cumulative and severe adverse impact that has never been taken into consideration in decision-making by the DLNR or Kawaiahaʻo Church.

D. DLNR Has Not Conducted the Historic Preservation Review Required by Its Own Rules

1. DLNR Has Violated HAR §§13-284-3(b)(1) and 13-284-5: An Archaeological Inventory Survey Is Required. The DLNR has failed to identify and inventory the "historic properties" that are present, as required in HAR §13-284-3(b)(1). By HAR §13-284-5, the DLNR has two basic choices: (1) issue a letter concluding that no significant historic sites are likely to be present or (2) require the project to undergo an "inventory survey" to determine if historic properties are present. When historic properties "may" be present or are "likely" to be present, an inventory survey must be prepared. In this particular case, it could not be clearer that historic properties are likely to be present.

The DLNR fails to recognize that the Kawaiahaʻo Church and Mission House were placed on the National Register of Historic Places on October 15, 1966, and that the Hawaiʻi Capital Historic District, including the Kawaiahaʻo property, was placed on the National Register of Historic Places on December 1, 1978. Thus the Kawaiahaʻo Church property is a "historic site" or "historic property."

When Kawaiahaʻo Church first presented the Multi-Purpose Center Project to DLNR, DLNR required the preparation of an Archaeological Inventory Survey (AIS) through a letter written by Ms. Holly McEldowney on behalf of the DLNR-SHPD, dated February 10, 2004. Agents of Kawaiahaʻo Church thereafter represented to DLNR that new construction would be contained within the footprint of the demolished Likeke Hall and that an underground parking structure would be eliminated, in part because excavation for the parking structure would potentially destabilize the foundation of the church. Based upon this new commitment, DLNR thereafter deleted its requirement for an AIS.

It is now clear that the footprint for the construction of the new Multi-Purpose Center will significantly exceed the footprint for the demolished Likeke Hall and office building. As such, there is no longer any factual basis for deleting the original DLNR requirement for the preparation of an AIS. Furthermore, an AIS should have been required from the start based upon the plans to trench for infrastructure construction. The DLNR must now reinstate the requirement for the preparation of an AIS prior to any further construction activities on the property.

The DLNR also fails to recognize that in April 2005 it was determined that it was "highly probable . . . that some burials or human bones were missed during the 1940 disinterments." The CSH report goes on to state that "it is also possible that there are precontact burials within the churchyard" (O'Hare 2005, 49).

Finally, "The Archaeological Monitoring Plan for the Kawaiahaʻo Church Ancillary Facilities Project, Kawaiahaʻo, Kona District, Oʻahu, TMK [1] 1-2-1-032:017" prepared for Kawaiahaʻo Church by Cultural Surveys Hawaiʻi Inc., dated August 2006, finds and concludes: "*Historic properties may be found anywhere within the project area*" (emphasis added). This determination compels the preparation of an AIS before any further construction activities take place on the Kawaiahaʻo Church property.

2. The Remainder of the Review Is Therefore Defective. The DLNR never evaluated the significance of these Native Hawaiian burials as significant historic properties, as required by HAR §13-284-3(b)(2).

The DLNR never determined the impact of the construction of the Multi-Purpose Center and the associated infrastructural improvements on these Native Hawaiian burials, as required by HAR §13-284-3(b)(3).

The DLNR never considered mitigation commitments and measures to minimize adverse impacts to these burials, as required by HAR §13-284-3(b)(4).

As importantly, the DLNR never afforded interested persons an opportunity to comment on the submittal's acceptability, as required by HAR §13-284-3(f). At a bare minimum, the O'ahu Island Burial Council should have been given the opportunity to comment. Instead, meetings were held at DLNR's offices with representatives of the DOH, SHPD including Pua Aiu and Nancy McMahon, and Kawaiaha'o Church, but not representatives of the O'ahu Island Burial Council.

E. Kawaiaha'o Is Not a Cemetery as That Word Is Used in HRS Chapter 441 and HRS §6E-41

Cemeteries must be dedicated to cemetery purposes, pursuant to HRS Chapter 441. Burial plots are sold or assigned to persons in perpetuity subject to terms and conditions. One term may be the conditions under which disinterment and relocation may occur. Records are kept of interments.

Operators of cemeteries have full knowledge of all those who are interred within the land areas covered by the burial plots. Cemetery operators are able to directly notify the relatives of those buried in the land areas covered by the burial plots of any important actions planned with respect to the cemetery or the particular burial plot or any persons interred within the land covered by the burial plot. If a cemetery operator wishes to relocate the cemetery, it has records indicating who the family members are of all those who are buried within the land covered by a burial plot. Based upon its records and its clear knowledge of exactly who is buried on its property, a cemetery operator is able to directly notify family members of any proposed decision to relocate the cemetery.

In this case, DOH was correct in attempting to require Kawaiaha'o Church to provide death certificates and the names of each individual that it wished to disinter and relocate. Kawaiaha'o Church objected because it was unable to provide this information for the individuals that it disinterred and proposes to disinter.

Kawaiaha'o Church may have operated a cemetery in the past

during a distinct period of time in its long history. The 1912 and 1920 Cemetery Maps indicate that the church laid out burial plots at this approximate time and through some process assigned these burial plots to church members. These church members interred their dead in these burial plots. The foregoing all show that the church was operating a cemetery for its members at these points in time.

Kawaiahaʻo Church no longer operates a cemetery. No plots are assigned to church members. The heirs of those assigned burial plots cannot bury their dead in the assigned burial plots. Kawaiahaʻo Church has not designated these areas as a cemetery pursuant to Chapter 441, to my knowledge.

Of greatest importance, however, is the fact that the Kawaiahaʻo Church property was a burial site for Native Hawaiians during lengthy precontact and postcontact periods of time, quite apart from the period of time the church may have subjected the property to its burial plot plans. The Kawaiahaʻo Church property contains precontact Native Hawaiian burials as well as historic period burials.

Kawaiahaʻo Church has long been fully aware of the use of its property as a burial site for Native Hawaiians during both the precontact and the postcontact periods. Based upon current evidence, these precontact and postcontact Native Hawaiian burials exist throughout the church property and even within the areas covered by the 1912 and 1920 Cemetery Maps, excepting the Mission Cemetery.

Unlike a cemetery, however, the church apparently has no detailed records of anything like assigned burial lots for these burials. The church has no idea who all the individuals are who are buried on its property. The church has no idea where precisely all these precontact and postcontact Native Hawaiian burials exist on its property, except through the major excavations that have taken place. Kawaiahaʻo Church has no idea which family members to notify about decisions regarding preservation in place or relocation with relation to these burial sites.

F. The Burials That Are the Subject Matter of Your Determination Are Not in a "Known, Maintained, Actively Used Cemetery"

Your determination that some of the burials at Kawaiahaʻo were in a "known" cemetery has no support. You were not able to find, as you were required to find, that these burials exist in a "known, maintained, actively used cemetery." Many of the burials at Kawaiahaʻo exist outside of any areas that could possibly be construed as a cemetery. Kawaiahaʻo Church has not "maintained" any cemetery for these particular burials. None of the normal indicia for known cemeteries are present for the areas that are the subject of your determination. Kawaiahaʻo Church has no cemetery area that it "actively uses" for these particular burials. Kawaiahaʻo Church has not dedicated these areas to cemetery purposes pursuant to HRS Chapter 441. There is no restriction in Kawaiahaʻo Church's deed, of which I am aware, that restricts these portions of the church's property to cemetery purposes alone. Kawaiahaʻo Church receives no tax exemption, of which I am aware, for dedicating these particular areas to cemetery purposes.

In fact, the areas in which these burials are located are not preserved for burial purposes at all. Anyone viewing the areas that are the subject of your determination would have no idea that the area is a cemetery. There is no signage indicating that the area is a cemetery. No headstones or other surface grave monuments are present. No area is fenced off or separated out for cemetery purposes. Those viewing these areas would see that these areas are in fact dedicated to noncemetery purposes instead. These areas were located underneath buildings actively used for other purposes. These areas are located beneath paved parking areas and paved access roadways.

Again, this determination was not only erroneous, it has also deprived me and others of the substantive and procedural due process rights conferred by the state burial law. By this determination, you suggest that the DOH can issue permits allowing the disinterment of these burials and their relocation elsewhere. DOH has no substantive standards that it must first apply to determine whether the law requires that the burials must remain in place. DOH has no substantive standards that it must first apply before it can authorize the disinterment of these burials and authorize their relocation elsewhere. Your erroneous determination has denied me and many others procedural and substantive due process in this respect as well.

G. The Burials Are Previously Identified

The determination that some of the burials at Kawaiahaʻo were "inadvertent discoveries" has no support, especially in view of the numerous prior historical and archaeological documents—of which either you were or should have been aware—indicating that burials existed throughout the Kawaiahaʻo property. Again, this determination was not only erroneous, it has also deprived me and others of the substantive and procedural due process rights conferred by the state burial law.

In particular, at the request of Kawaiahaʻo Church, CSH conducted limited inventory survey subsurface testing on Kawaiahaʻo Church property in 2006 and documented the results in *An Archaeological Subsurface Investigation at Kawaiahaʻo Church Cemetery, Honolulu Ahupuaʻa, Kona District, Island of Oʻahu TMK: (1) 2-1-032: 016 and 017* (Tulchin and Hammatt 2006). A total of *twenty-four (24) burials* were identified on Kawaiahaʻo Church property during this very limited archaeological inventory investigation. Burials identified in AISs, such as this one, prior to construction activities, are "previously identified" by law. *These "previously identified" burials have never been reported by DLNR or Kawaiahaʻo Church to the Oʻahu Island Burial Council for proper treatment and disposition*. A Burial Treatment Plan, long overdue, must be prepared for these burials and presented for a determination by the Oʻahu Island Burial Council, pursuant to HAR §13-300-33.

Some troubling issues are presented by this matter. First, these 24 burials are undisputedly located in the project area. HAR §13-276-2 defines project area as:

> the area the proposed project may potentially affect, either directly or indirectly. It includes not only the area where the project will take place, but also the proposed project's area of potential effect.

Next, HAR §13-276-3 states that an archaeological inventory, generally, shall:

> (1) Determine if archaeological historic properties are present in the project area and, if so, identify all such historic properties.
>
> (2) Gather sufficient information to evaluate each historic property's significance in accordance with the criteria listed in section 13-275-6(b).

In this case, historic properties, notably 24 burials presumably unknown until the 2006 test excavations, were found to be present in the project area.

As such, the 24 burials are classified as "previously identified." The definition of previously identified, according to HAR §13-300-2,

> means burial sites containing human skeletal remains and any burial goods identified during archaeological inventory survey and data recovery of possible burial sites, or known through written or oral testimony.

The archaeological subsurface investigation conducted in 2006 was certainly a limited AIS in that it was conducted in an area that had not been subjected to inventory-level survey in the past, and the exploration resulted in the determination that historic properties (that is, burials) are present. Furthermore, the report produced on the results of this archaeological work constitutes written testimony.

H. Comments on the June 11, 2006, Historic Preservation Review Letter from Laura Thielen to Donald Caindec

1. Deprived Interested Persons of Notice and Opportunity to Participate. On June 11, 2009, Ms. Thielen, as DLNR chair (and State Historic Preservation Officer) wrote a letter to Donald Caindec of Kawaiahaʻo Church that outlines guidelines on how to proceed with the Multi-Purpose Center project "and provide a respectful disinterment and final resting place for the ʻiwi [*sic*] kupuna in your care."

This letter makes reference to the Archaeological Monitoring Plan (AMP) prepared by CSH and submitted to the SHPD in August 2006. I was able to obtain a copy of this plan only two days ago; I was not aware of its existence until a week ago, since I had no notice of its receipt by the SHPD in 2006. Neither this AMP, the April 2005 *Background Information in Support of Subsurface Testing, Monitoring and Burial Treatment Plans for the Kawaiahaʻo Church Ancillary Facility Project, Honolulu Ahupuaʻa, Kawaiahaʻo ʻIli, Kona District, Island of Oʻahu* (O'Hare 2005), nor a 2006 report titled *An Archaeological Subsurface Investigation at Kawaiahaʻo Church Cemetery* (Shideler 2006) —all of which were prepared by Cultural Surveys Hawaiʻi Inc.— were made available by the DLNR-SHPD to interested persons and the general public for comment.

The DLNR-SHPD failed to post a notice of SHPD receipt of these documents as required by HAR §13-284-3(f). The great majority of historic preservation review for this project has been conducted outside of the view and without the participation of all interested persons and the public, and at cross-purposes with the intent of Chapter 6E, Hawaiʻi's historic preservation law.

2. History of Kawaiahaʻo Cemeteries. This section of the June 11 letter states: "In the last reconstruction of Likeke Hall in 1940 . . . the church believed it removed and reinterred any burials at the location of the existing Likeke Hall." This statement is erroneous and confusing. The 2006 CSH monitoring plan (pp. 45 and 53) discusses the 1940 preparations undertaken by the church for the construction of Likeke Hall. Likeke Hall was constructed in 1940–41, not reconstructed.

3. Appropriate Jurisdiction—6E-41, Hawaiʻi Revised Statutes. DLNR's letter asserts that "state law contains a provision that addresses the treatment of burials in cemeteries where *the graves are no longer marked or identified*" (emphasis added). You claim that this provision, HRS §6E-41, treats these unidentified burials the same as burials whose identities are known in any known cemetery. This is a misreading of §6E-41. For instance, §6E-41(2) states, "take separate photographs of all *headstones* located in the cemetery" and §6E-41(4) states, "move all *headstones* to the place of reinterment." There is nothing in this section of the statute that directly addresses unmarked or unidentified graves.

4. Prior Example—Nāwiliwili Cemetery. You next cite the example of the removal of Nāwiliwili Cemetery, twenty years ago in 1989, under HRS §6E-41. May I remind you that this example does not appear to be relevant, since this removal occurred prior to the establishment of the burial statute, §6E-43.

5. Departmental Roles. This section of Ms. Thielen's letter contains the following statement: "Under §338-25.5, HRS, the Director of the Department of Health is authorized to provide *disinterment permits for known burials*" (emphasis added). Kawaiaha'o Church, the applicant for the disinterment permit, does not know the identities of the individuals whose remains they seek to remove and relocate, therefore, DOH does not have jurisdiction over these unknown burials.

The letter goes on to state that the DLNR's rules "allow for the disinterment of unidentified burials, to set conditions on the removal of an existing cemetery." What the letter fails to include is language in HRS §338-25.5(b) that clarifies that the DLNR may "authorize exposure, removal, disinterment, or any other act without obtaining a permit from the Department of Health," but only pursuant to §6E-43 and §6E-43.6. Invoking the legal authority of §6E-43 and §6E-43.6 brings into play the rules of practice and procedure relating to burial sites and human remains. The DLNR cannot ignore the substantive criteria and procedures contained in its own rules, which are in place to protect burial sites and to recognize their significance.

6. Permit Conditions. Ms. Thielen's letter outlines conditions for a five-phase process as the SHPD's "proposed mitigation and conditional concurrence with the proposed disinterment permit to be provided by the Department of Health."

Phase I—Consultation. In order to conduct meaningful consultation with descendants, if any, the O'ahu Island Burial Council,

OHA, Hui Mālama I Nā Kūpuna O Hawai'i Nei, and other interested persons—full-size, to-scale construction plans must be available for review. In addition, information on the width, length, and depth of trenches to be excavated for new utilities, and their routes, must be made available. The proposed project plans should be shown within the context of the entire property. The locations of all previously identified historic properties and sites on Kawaiaha'o property also should be shown in relation to construction activities.

Phase II—Low Impact. Additional ground penetrating radar (GPR) was to be conducted. However, since Kawaiaha'o elected to remove all burials from the construction site, the SHPD and Kawaiaha'o decided that further GPR work would be unnecessary. This condition is objectionable, since it illegally predetermines relocation for any burials encountered. According to this scheme, there is no provision for the option to preserve in place, in violation of HRS §6E-43 and the administrative rules.

Phase III—Subsurface. Again, this condition only contemplates removal of all burials and thus the condition does not comport with the burial statute rules. It gave me a chill to read about the requirement for submittal of a weekly progress report to the SHPD. A similar condition was attached to the approval to disinter the Honokahua Burial Site.

Phase IV—Construction. This condition refers to an archaeological monitoring plan submitted to and approved by the SHPD on September 26, 2006. The letter states that this plan is still valid and is amended only with respect to stating that the archaeological monitoring activity will be under HRS §6E-41. There is no provision for archaeological monitoring under §6E-41. The letter also makes reference to the "69 inadvertent burials, outside the cemetery boundaries and treated under §6E-42 H.R.S." This reference is incorrect. I believe that what is meant is §6E-43.6. I do not agree with this determination for reasons stated earlier.

Phase V—Burial Treatment. The June 11 letter declares that a final report approved by the SHPD "shall constitute burial treatment for unmarked human remains which are to be relocated to the active

Kawaiaha'o Church Cemetery." A request for council or department (whichever is relevant) determination to preserve or relocate Native Hawaiian burial sites is submitted in the form of a BTP (HAR §§13-300-33 and 34). There is no provision in the burial statute of the rules for "a final report" constituting burial treatment.

The letter ends by stating: "We look forward to working with you to ensure the long-term protection of these unmarked burials"—an ironic statement, to say the least.

II. The DLNR and DOH Do Not Possess the Legal Authority to Disinter Burials at Kawaiaha'o Church in the Manner Suggested in the Letter Dated June 11, 2009

The authority of DOH to disinter is found in HRS §338-25.5(a), which states with respect to the "Disinterment of human bodies":

> (a) No corpse, nor the remains of any dead human body, exclusive of ashes, shall be exposed, disturbed, or removed from its place of burial, nor shall the receptacle, container, or coffin holding the remains or corpse be opened, removed, or disturbed after due interment, except upon written application made to the director of health for a permit therefore and upon the issuance and according to the terms of a permit granted therefore by the director. After any removal or disturbance the grave shall be filled at once and restored to its former condition.

By 1990, DOH only retained the authority to authorize the disinterment of nonhistoric burials or burials existing in "a known, maintained, actively used cemetery." See HRS §§6E-43, 338-23 and 338-25.

As of 1990, the disinterment of historic burials, outside of "a known, maintained, actively used cemetery," could only be authorized pursuant to HRS §§6E-43 and 6E-43.6, as HRS §338-25.5 recognizes:

> (b) Notwithstanding the provisions of subsection (a), the department of land and natural resources *pursuant to sections 6E-43 and 6E-43.6* may authorize exposure, removal, disinterment, or any other act without obtaining a permit from the department of health. (Emphasis added)

HRS §6E-43, titled "Prehistoric and historic burial sites," states:

(a) At any site, other than a known, maintained, actively used cemetery where human skeletal remains are discovered or are known to be buried and appear to be over fifty years old, the remains and their associated burial goods shall not be moved without the department's approval.

(b) *All burial sites are significant and shall be preserved in place until compliance with this section is met, except as provided in section 6E-43.6. The appropriate island burial council shall determine whether preservation in place or relocation of previously identified native Hawaiian burial sites is warranted, following criteria which shall include recognition that burial sites of high preservation value, such as areas with a concentration of skeletal remains, or prehistoric or historic burials associated with important individuals and events, or areas that are within a context of historic properties, or have known lineal descendants, shall receive greater consideration for preservation in place.* The criteria shall be developed by the department in consultation with the councils, Office of Hawaiian Affairs, representatives of development and large property owner interests, and appropriate Hawaiian organizations, such as Hui Mālama I Nā Kūpuna O Hawai'i Nei, through rules adopted pursuant to chapter 91. A council's determination shall be rendered within forty-five days of referral by the department unless otherwise extended by agreement between the landowner and the department.

(c) Within ninety days following the final determination, a preservation or mitigation plan shall be approved by the department in consultation with any lineal descendants, the respective council, other appropriate Hawaiian organizations, and any affected property owner. (Emphasis added)

HRS §6E-43.6, titled "Inadvertent discovery of burial sites," states:

(a) In the event human skeletal remains are inadvertently discovered, any activity in the immediate area that could damage the remains or the potential historic site shall cease until the requirements of subsections (b) to (d) have been met.

(b) The discovery shall be reported as soon as possible to the department, the appropriate medical examiner or coroner, and the appropriate police department. As soon as practicable, *the department shall notify the appropriate council and the Office of Hawaiian Affairs.*

(c) After notification of the discovery of multiple skeletons, the following shall be done within two working days, if on Oʻahu, and three working days, if in other council jurisdictions:

(1) A representative of the medical examiner or coroner's office and a qualified archaeologist shall examine the remains to determine jurisdiction. If the remains are the responsibility of the medical examiner or coroner, the department's involvement shall end. If the remains are historic or prehistoric burials, then the remainder of this section shall apply;

(2) The department shall gather sufficient information, including oral tradition, to document the nature of the burial context and determine appropriate treatment of the remains. *Members of the appropriate council shall be allowed to oversee the on-site examination* and, if warranted, removal; and

(3) *If removal of the remains is warranted, based on criteria developed by the department, in consultation with the councils*, Office of Hawaiian Affairs, representatives of development and large property owner interests, and appropriate Hawaiian organizations, such as Hui Mālama I Nā Kūpuna O Hawaiʻi Nei, *through rules adopted pursuant to chapter 91*, the removal of the remains shall be overseen by a qualified archaeologist and a mitigation plan shall be prepared by the department or with the concurrence of the department. (Emphasis added)

(d) In cases involving the discovery of a single skeleton, the requirements of subsection (c) shall be fulfilled in one working day if on Oʻahu, and two working days if in other council jurisdictions.

(e) The mitigation plan developed by or with the concurrence of the department pursuant to subsection (c)(3) shall be carried out in accordance with the following:

(1) In discoveries related to development where land alteration project activities exist, the landowner, permittee, or developer shall be responsible for the execution of the mitigation plan including relocation of remains. Justifiable delays resulting from the discovery of burials shall not count against any contractor's completion date agreement;

(2) Project activities shall resume once necessary archaeological excavations provided in the mitigation plan have been completed;

(3) In nonproject contexts, the department shall be responsible for the execution of the mitigation plan and the relocation of remains; and

(4) The department shall verify the successful execution of the mitigation plan.

(f) In cases where remains are archaeologically removed, the department shall determine the place of relocation, after consultation with the appropriate council, affected property owners, representatives of the relevant ethnic group, and any identified lineal descendants, as appropriate. Relocation shall conform with requirements imposed by the department of health, and may be accompanied by traditional ceremonies, as determined by the lineal descendants, or, if no lineal descendants are identified, the appropriate council or representatives of the relevant ethnic group that the department deems appropriate. Specific or special reinterment requests from lineal or cultural descendants may be accommodated provided that the additional expenses incurred are paid by the affected descendants.

(g) If human skeletal remains are discovered in the course of land development or land alteration activities to which section 6E-42 applies, and for which the required approval was not obtained, all activity in the immediate area that could damage the remains or the potential historic site shall cease, and treatment of the remains shall be allowed only in compliance with section 6E-43.

If disinterment occurs unlawfully, Kawaiahaʻo Church, DLNR and DOH can be subject to statutory penalties pursuant to HRS §338-30:

(a) Except where a different penalty is provided in this part, any person who violates this part, or neglects or refuses to perform any of the duties imposed upon the person by this part, shall be fined not more than $100.

(b) Any person who willfully makes or alters any certificate or certified copy thereof provided for in this part except in accordance with this part, shall be fined not more than $1,000, or imprisoned not more than six months, or both.

> (c) Any person, who knowingly transports, or accepts for transportation, interment, or other disposition, a dead body without an accompanying permit issued in accordance with this part, shall be fined not more than $500.
>
> (d) Any person who presents false information in order to obtain access to or a certified copy of a vital record for which the person is not eligible is guilty of a misdemeanor and shall be fined not more than $1,000.

III. Agencies Cannot Permit Any Further Construction Activities on the Kawaiahaʻo Church Property until the Environmental Process Is Lawfully Concluded

A. An Environmental Assessment Is Required for the Proposed Kawaiahaʻo Church Multi-Purpose Center Project

HRS §343-5(a) provides that:

> Except as otherwise provided, an environmental assessment shall be required for actions that: . . .
> (4) Propose any use within any historic site as designated in the National Register or Hawaiʻi Register, as provided for in the Historic Preservation Act of 1966, Public Law 89-665, or chapter 6E;

The Kawaiahaʻo Church and the Hawaiian Mission Houses were placed on the National Register of Historic Places on October 15, 1966. The Hawaiʻi Capital Historic District was placed on the National Register of Historic Places on December 1, 1978. This district encompasses many properties, including the Kawaiahaʻo property. The entire Kawaiahaʻo property is therefore a "historic site." As such, a "triggering event" requiring the preparation of an EA was and is present for the proposed Kawaiahaʻo Church MPC project.

HRS §343-5(c) further states:

> Whenever an applicant proposes an action specified by subsection (a) that requires approval of an agency and that is not a specific type of action declared exempt under section 343-6, the agency initially receiving and agreeing to process the request for approval shall pre-

pare an environmental assessment of the proposed action at the earliest practicable time to determine whether an environmental impact statement shall be required.

No exemption determination has been entered by any agency with regard to the proposed Kawaiahaʻo Church Multi-Purpose Center project to my knowledge. Therefore, by HRS §343-5(c), an EA is required to be prepared for this project.

B. Discretionary Approvals Are Required for the Proposed Kawaiahaʻo Church Multi-Purpose Center Project

There are a number of permits or approvals that must be issued by agencies prior to the implementation of the proposed Kawaiahaʻo Church Multi-Purpose Center project, including the following of which I am currently aware:

- Decision of the Oʻahu Island Burial Council on whether the Native Hawaiian burials should be preserved in place, as a matter of law, or whether they may be relocated to make way for the proposed Kawaiahaʻo Church Multi-Purpose Center;
- Approval of HCDA for the proposed Kawaiahaʻo Church Multi-Purpose Center;
- Approval of DLNR of the historic preservation review, pursuant to HRS §6E-42, for the proposed Kawaiahaʻo Church Multi-Purpose Center;
- Trenching permits issued by Department of Planning and Permitting, City and County of Honolulu to install the infrastructure for the proposed Kawaiahaʻo Church Multi-Purpose Center project;
- Building permit issued by Department of Planning and Permitting, City and County of Honolulu, to construct the proposed Kawaiahaʻo Church Multi-Purpose Center; and
- In the alternative, DOH permit issued by DOH to disinter Native Hawaiian burials to make way for the proposed Kawaiahaʻo Church Multi-Purpose Center.

C. An Environmental Assessment Must Now Be Prepared before the Proposed Kawaiahaʻo Church Multi-Purpose Center Project Is Implemented Any Further

All of the discretionary permits or approvals for the proposed Kawaiahaʻo Church Multi-Purpose Center project have not yet been issued. Construction of the proposed Kawaiahaʻo Church Multi-Purpose Center itself has not yet commenced. Trenching activities for the infrastructure have ceased. This demand for compliance with HRS Chapter 343 and the preparation of an EA for the proposed Kawaiahaʻo Church Multi-Purpose Center is timely made. The following specific demands are made upon Kawaiahaʻo Church and the permitting and approving agencies to bring all of them immediately into compliance with Chapter 343:

- Begin preparation of an EA for the proposed Kawaiahaʻo Church Multi-Purpose Center. It is a mandatory requirement of HRS §343-5(c) that an EA be prepared at the "earliest practicable time" for the proposed Kawaiahaʻo Church Multi-Purpose Center. This EA must be prepared now.

- Cease further implementation of the proposed Kawaiahaʻo Church Multi-Purpose Center. HRS §343-5(b) provides that:

> Acceptance of a required final statement shall be a condition precedent to implementation of the proposed action.

This "condition precedent" language is also mandatory. The proposed Kawaiahaʻo Church Multi-Purpose Center cannot be further implemented until the environmental process is lawfully completed. Forbidding implementation of the project while the project undergoes environmental review places a hold on the project and on approvals, permits, and entitlements for the project. *Kepoo v. Watson (Kepoo I)*, 87 Haw. 91, 100-101, 952 P.2d 379 (1998); *Kepoo v. Kane (Kepoo II)*, 106 Haw. 270, 103 P.3d 939 (2005).

- Cease issuance of further permits or approvals for the proposed Kawaiahaʻo Church Multi-Purpose Center; and HAR §11-200-23(d) states that:

> Acceptance of the required EIS shall be a condition precedent to approval of the request and commencement of the proposed action.

Permits or approvals, including the DOH permit for disinterment, cannot be issued for the proposed Kawaiahaʻo Church Multi-Purpose Center project until the environmental process is lawfully completed.

- Revoke or void any existing permits or approvals for the proposed Kawaiahaʻo Church Multi-Purpose Center. Any permits or approvals issued prior to the lawful completion of the environmental process must be revoked or are void as a matter of law. *Sierra Club v. Office of Planning*, 109 Haw. 411, 126 P.3d 1089 (2006) and *KSOA v. County of Maui*, 86 Haw. 66, 947 P.2d 378 (1997).

I request that all addressees respond positively in writing by the close of business (4:30 p.m.) on July 16, 2009, agreeing that no further construction activities will be conducted on the Kawaiahaʻo property and no further permits will be issued until an Archaelogical Inventory Survey and an Environmental Assessment are completed. I look forward to your timely responses.

Sincerely,
Dana Naone Hall

Office of Hawaiian Affairs Board of Trustees Meeting 46

TESTIMONY BEFORE THE TRUSTEES
UNIVERSITY OF HAWAI'I MAUI COLLEGE
AUGUST 16, 2012

Good morning, Chair Machado and trustees. Thank you for coming to Maui (saving me a trip to Honolulu) and for the opportunity to follow up on a letter that I sent to the chair and administration two weeks ago concerning the disinterments at Kawaiahaʻo. I know that I have only a few minutes so I will be as concise as possible.

Kawaiahaʻo presents a moral, ethical, cultural, and spiritual challenge to all of us. This controversy has been stewing since early 2009 when it was reported that 69 individuals had been excavated for a sewer line to serve a proposed Multi-Purpose Center (MPC) project on church property. I won't go into the jurisdictional issues—there are two lawsuits pending—since my purpose today extends beyond the limits of those actions.

The Multi-Purpose Center building was projected to cost $17.5 million. As of the end of May 2012, $10.35 million has already been expended for the project with $1.58 million of that amount spent for archaeological and cultural services, primarily to facilitate the disinterment of burials. It would appear that the economic costs of the project are prohibitive, especially since the burial excavations have not been completed and further court action to decertify the MPC building area as a cemetery have not taken place—all of which must occur prior to any construction. At this point, it must be asked whether Kawaiahaʻo can reasonably be expected to build the MPC or whether other alternatives and options should be explored.

I am here to request the participation of the Office of Hawaiian Affairs (OHA) in reviewing and reassessing the current course of disinterments at Kawaiahaʻo. Earlier in the controversy, OHA endeavored to help resolve the dispute through hoʻoponopono. I am very grateful for that effort, which extended from late March to early December of 2011, even if we ultimately were unable to hoʻopono the matter of the proper care of the iwi kupuna.

While we were still engaged in hoʻoponopono, the church leadership decided to restart burial excavations. Upon resumption of digging, weekly reports filed by Cultural Surveys Hawaiʻi (CSH) in July and August of last year noted the finding of coffin burials and disturbed human skeletal remains not associated with the coffin burials. Also noted were concentrations of artifacts and numerous faunal remains, including pig, dog, and fish bones—a potential indication of traditional burials and burial practices.

The last reference to a coffin burial in the CSH weekly reports that I can find occurs in early October of last year. Thereafter, references to coffin burials cease and no information is included on findings of artifacts or faunal bones. The reports contain only the bare information of increasing burial numbers and what the reports refer to as "isolated finds" even when hundreds of human bones and bone fragments are collected from the same specific area.

The MPC site, currently enclosed by a high-security fence, encompasses approximately 0.56 acres or 24,500 square feet. By August 4, 2012, 572 burials had been excavated. The number of burials rises as the digging continues, adding to an already staggering concentration in little more than half an acre. The actual number of individuals whose remains have been collected exceeds 572. For example, the total number of burials recovered during the week of January 23 to January 28, 2012, is reported as 19, representing a minimum number of 25 individuals. Another burial find consisted of eight crania (skulls) buried together.

To help put these figures into perspective, the minimum number of individuals recovered from the Honokahua Burial Site was 1,029. An estimated 1,000 individuals were left undisturbed in the dune burial site, which, based on archaeological testing, was determined to be 3.07 acres in size. The burial concentration at Kawaiahaʻo is even denser than at Honokahua.

CSH's finding of precontact, traditional burials as well as traditional artifacts in the late 1980s during monitoring of Queen Street excavations immediately adjoining Kawaiahaʻo cemetery, and more recently CSH's recovery in 2002 of a precontact burial near the intersection of King and Punchbowl Streets, adjacent to Kawaiahaʻo Church property, strongly indicate the potential for finding precontact burials at Kawaiahaʻo. These modern findings support early historic missionary accounts of encountering native burials at Kawaiahaʻo.

In the past seven and one-half months alone, from January 2012 to the present, the remains of nearly 350 individuals have been taken from the Multi-Purpose Center site in addition to more than 4,000 bones and bone fragments. I strongly believe that some of the burials that have been encountered at Kawaiahaʻo are precontact, traditional burials not subject to the Department of Health blanket disinterment permit.

The Honokahua Burial Site was excavated under a DOH blanket disinterment permit. Twenty-five years ago, I and others sought OHA's assistance to prevent further digging at Honokahua. It is undisputed that any precontact burials encountered at Kawaiahaʻo cannot be disinterred pursuant to the DOH permit. Once again, I ask OHA's help in reassessing the situation at Kawaiahaʻo, specifically the issues of whether precontact burials have been found and, if so, whether the disinterments must now stop so that the kūpuna can continue to rest in peace.

A view of the excavations for the Multi-Purpose Center from a second-floor window of Kawaiahaʻo Church. The building just beyond the black construction fence is Kawaiahaʻo School.

Photograph by Claire Hiwahiwa Steele.

Press Statement on the Intermediate Court of Appeals Ruling in Favor of Plaintiff-Appellant in Kawaiahaʻo Case

SEPTEMBER 28, 2012

After three years of working through the courts (the lawsuit was filed in August 2009), the Intermediate Court of Appeals determined that "there is a substantial likelihood that we will conclude that the SHPD [State Historic Preservation Division] should have required Kawaiahaʻo Church to complete an AIS [Archaeological Inventory Survey] before state approval of the MPC [Multi-Purpose Center] project and that SHPD violated its own rules in failing to require an AIS before permitting the project to go forward."

Plaintiff-Appellant Dana Naone Hall said, "This case spans the end of the Lingle Administration and the first years of the Abercrombie Administration, during which time the SHPD has routinely failed to follow its own rules to the detriment of historic properties and burial sites. I am very grateful to the Intermediate Court of Appeals for reaffirming that there is a vital public interest in protecting human skeletal remains and burial sites 'regardless of race, religion, or cultural origin.' Although approximately 700 individuals have been disturbed at Kawaiahaʻo, there are many hundreds more who can continue to rest in peace."

Woman Warrior

48

EXCERPTS FROM "A HAWAIIAN WOMAN AND A WARRIOR," AN INTERVIEW IN *ISLAND CURRENTS*

FEBRUARY 1991

I was walking up here along a side street called Onaona, which means *fragrant*. It was so beautiful today, and it hit me again that the Hawai'i I love is disappearing—the Hawai'i that's within reach, where you're surrounded by reminders of what the islands really are. I'm not interested in having pockets of more or less wild places left where every now and then you can make an excursion that amounts to a pilgrimage—a little bit of lowland rain forest, something on top of the West Maui Mountains, a crater . . . that's not enough! When we begin to urbanize and suburbanize our landscape, we really erase what's Hawaiian about the place. I think that if people realize it's not an inevitable process, they might wish to do more about it.

I don't think you can deal with land issues in Hawai'i without being aware of the mana, the spiritual power, that's inherent in the land. When you see something that's disfiguring the body of the place you love (for instance, Maui), then, in some very real way, that is a disfigurement of yourself. It's a signal that other people, other forces don't think in terms of respect for the land itself, or are not interested in doing things for it that are beneficial, in the traditional sense. It's more important for them to destroy something that exists in order to re-create something else that's going to make them more money. That's not a very Hawaiian value. So, as modern-day Hawaiians, we have some very severe conflicts, watching this occurring on our islands.

It's not a game for people with economic interests. I try not to see just us and them. That prevents you from seeing all the options. The more you solidify the positions, the less able you are to be fluid; you've got to be able to try to look at and understand what's going on with the other side, not just from a tactical point of view but from a human point of view. You have to try to stay open.

I felt that I could say things for people and places that couldn't speak for themselves. What are you going to do when somebody comes in and starts changing your home around without your permission? You feel impelled. It's not "As long as I have my carpets and my vertical blinds, I'm cool." It's like the American Indians who speak of the whole of nature as their church. In that sense, the whole of the islands is my home. When people come, they are entering someone's home. It's a very traditional concept. You have to be deferential to your host.

When the whole system worked, it was reciprocal. You would never dream of accepting something without returning something. Everybody had something, because everyone was engaged in the act of giving. Giving the best of what you have dies out if it's not a complete circuit. Some people act as if Polynesian cultures are supposed to be completely openhanded, to the point where we're supposed to give away the whole island so it can become a playground.

In the Hawaiian movement, there is a tradition of the warrior. But, you know, women fought too in the old battles. I myself feel I have a warrior-like mentality. I don't mind getting into a fight with government entities or developers. I have a lot of stamina. There's a lot of doomsday saying, but I don't believe it. You've got to do what you've got to do. One thing it has taught me is you can't be a crybaby—either I have to win, or else it's not worth it—whatever winning means. You have to go in dedicating yourself, no matter what the outcome. That's the nature of it.

We want to make sure Hawaiian sites are not just an echo of time past but things that have meaning to us right now and are part of a continuum—something that began in a time when no one was counting, and coming up to right now and going ahead of us into our future, that's what we want.

You honor your past and you prepare for your future. And it's not even an exclusively Hawaiian picture. There are others I love who are not Hawaiian. For all of us. But what is Hawaiian about the place deserves to be protected and preserved.

The Cave

When I was younger I argued
about Chinese food with my boyfriend
a surfer from California.
What about exactly I don't remember
but like a wok spitting hot oil
I said, "Don't argue with me
about something you can't possibly
know better." During those years
I had a teacher who was small
and dark and finely featured.
He knew something of life's dark
mysteries and he knew about poetry.
To gain knowledge one had to do
more than sit at his feet. While he
meditated in the next room I cooked
omelettes and roasted a duck once
to sustain his frail ethereal presence
He was angry when I moved on
to learn at the knee of a better poet.
This time I traveled farther
than I ever had before. I lived
for a time in an apartment six
floors above an avenue of cars.
On my first night in the city
we went for a walk in the stunned light
and arrived at a Japanese restaurant.
I ate like a condemned person.
I knew I would have to stumble

into the street the next day on my own
past the place where the long loaves
slid out of the oven and into
the window of the Italian bakery
past the meat shop with the sheep's
head on a hook past the rows of Atlantic
fish on dull ice to the fruit stands
where car exhaust covered
the apples like a second skin.
Back along the avenues I came
with my bags to climb the marble
stairs to the steel door at the top.
After seven years I returned
to my island. For a while
I lived high off the ground
like the clear water in a coconut.
Then the night bird called
and I left the sloping valley behind.
We found the cave
on the mountain where the ash
from countless fires is still visible.
The sun is already high in the sky.
At the mouth of the cave
the Ancestress beckons
offering food, offering water
a place in the shade
to the passing travelers.

Sovereign Ground

50

RETHINKING THE WAY FORWARD: OLA NĀ IWI

Protests erupted over the excavation of an ancient Hawaiian burial site at Honokahua, Maui, in October 1988; by December of that year, Governor John Waiheʻe halted the digging. Honokahua represented the first time that massive desecration and destruction of a burial site had been stopped. The disturbed remains of 1,100 individuals, which archaeologists estimated represented about half the number of those buried there, were reinterred at the site, and out of that sacrifice, Hawaiʻi's burial protection law was born.

Honokahua was not the first large-scale disturbance of a sand dune burial site, given the penchant for building hotels on Hawaiʻi's shorelines. Stories still abound about the earlier development of Kāʻanapali, several miles south of Kapalua, and one can only imagine the displacement of thousands of ancient graves in Waikīkī. However, the point of this reflection is not to mourn what is gone, but to move forward with the understanding that it is possible to renew our connection to the past and rethink the future.

Hawaiʻi's postcontact history is filled with episodes of Native Hawaiians' alienation from the land to the point where many of our people are homeless today—both those forced to live on beaches or under freeways and those unable to afford the price of a house and consigned to rent other people's houses for the rest of their lives.

The alienation of land through its acquisition and development by others (in the case of hotel development, by out-of-state and, frequently, international entities) compels a deeper understanding of the past.

Since Honokahua, I have encountered hundreds of ancestral burials and the funerary objects that sometimes accompany them. Some of the burials are a thousand years old and more, while others date from the fifteenth to nineteenth centuries. Our state burial law declares that all burial sites are significant, and this statute is weighted toward preservation in place of these sites. Each site, whether found alone or among a concentration of burials, is unique.

No one owns a burial site except perhaps the individual whose remains are interred at that site. Importantly, not even a landowner owns the burials that may be present on property he or she owns. This fundamental fact gives the burial places of our Hawaiian ancestors an inherent sovereignty.

Wherever our Hawaiian ancestors are buried, an island of sovereignty exists. Each time a decision is made to disinter Hawaiian iwi from their place of burial, their home for numberless years, our right to exist is affected. On the other hand, every decision to preserve in place a Native Hawaiian burial site strengthens us as a people.

In recent years, the State Historic Preservation Division (SHPD) has allowed politics and economic demands to trump laws and administrative rules designed to protect and preserve significant cultural and historic sites for future generations. One high-profile case involved the redevelopment of the Ward Villages property in Kaka'ako. More than sixty burials were identified during the course of subsurface excavations, and many of these burials were disturbed or completely disinterred during initial phases of the project.

A number of the burials were found in a sandy matrix that composed the original sand dune system. I was amazed that beneath urban fill the iwi had slept undisturbed in the dunes until now. For me, this was history at its most intimate. But, just as we were rediscovering these ancient vestiges, they were being destroyed.

The poignancy of this situation was underscored by another bit of history. The land once belonged to Victoria Ward (born in 1846) and her family. Victoria Ward was a great supporter of the Hawaiian monarchy and remained a loyal friend to Queen Liliʻuokalani after the overthrow. As an expression of her sentiments she slept under a Hawaiian flag attached to the canopy of her bed.

While I believe that serious mistakes were made in the Ward Villages case and that SHPD was derelict in its duties, nevertheless, Honokahua, as its name indicates, has given us the opportunity to make our foundation stronger. As living descendants, we honor those who placed the iwi in their resting places with the intent that they remain undisturbed throughout time. Fulfilling this responsibility, we reaffirm who we are as a people—that we too have a place here, and it comes from the bones of our ancestors.

THE PRICE OF PARADISE REDUX

Hawaiʻi ranks first in state tourism spending among the fifty states. As the fourth smallest state in area, it might be said that more money is spent per acre to market Hawaiʻi than any other state. Hawaiʻi also spends more per visitor. In 2009, Hawaiʻi spent $60 million to draw 6.5 million tourists. California, the third largest state, expended $50 million to capture 28 million visitors. Florida, twenty-second largest, paid $13.5 million and attracted 94.7 million visitors.

Even though tourism revenue accounts for nearly 30 percent of Hawaiʻi's gross state product, the comparative figures given above argue for a rethinking of the commitment of so much public money for this industry. Most political candidates dutifully recite the need to diversify our economy without any real follow-up. If we are serious, a community-wide public discussion must be undertaken and priorities for state spending must be shifted. Otherwise, Hawaiʻi will continue to be buffeted by economic winds and global events beyond its control.

THE EDUCATION OF HAWAIIAN CHILDREN

Everyone has a stake in the education of Hawaiʻi's children. Kamehameha Schools has a particular stake in the education of children of

Hawaiian ancestry. In the years that I attended Kamehameha, there was only the Kapālama campus on the island of O'ahu.

Soon after decisions were made to construct new schools on Maui and the island of Hawai'i, the Bishop Estate trustees, charged with implementing the will of Bernice Pauahi Bishop, became engulfed in controversy. One of the trustees was a former district superintendent of public schools on Maui; she was known as the "education" trustee. Education was her fiefdom and she ruled with an autocratic hand.

I felt, at that time, that if new schools were to be built on neighbor islands the emphasis should be on educating orphans and the indigent, as Princess Bernice, or Ke Ali'i Pauahi as she is now referred to, intended. I have always hoped that after Kapālama the trust's resources would be directed toward educating the least advantaged of our children.

With the majority of the state's population residing on O'ahu, gathering approximately 3,000 academically gifted Hawaiian students at the Kapālama campus (including students from outer islands who boarded at the school) did not impoverish other schools, whether public or private, of academically successful native Hawaiian student role models. This is not the case on Hawai'i Island and Maui. There is a much more insular quality to these campuses, and while I do not begrudge these fine students the opportunities presented to them, I cannot help but feel that as the "best and brightest" they were likely to be successful at whatever school they chose to attend, and in the public school context, they would have added to the vitality of these schools.

The more difficult decision would be to educate the underserved. It may not be as attractive to take on the task of addressing learning disabilities and learning delays, but surely it can be just as rewarding. We have one bright, shining academy on a hill. Did we really need two more?

I know and appreciate that Kamehameha Schools offers a number of important outreach programs, but what I am advocating is not the provision of limited, intermittent services, but a comprehensive and sustained effort to serve those for whom a meaningful education, and its attendant opportunities, are out of reach.

LIVING IN A SOVEREIGN LAND

In 1990, the sale of Molokai Ranch to a Hong Kong firm was completed. I wished, at the time, that the purchase of one-third of the island's land (55,680 acres or 87 square miles) had been accomplished by the Office of Hawaiian Affairs (OHA)—the price seemed reasonable enough to be within OHA's reach.

The sovereignty debate had long been raging, and I thought that what was needed was a land base where sovereignty could actually be practiced. Moloka'i seemed suited to this endeavor because traditional and customary subsistence practices are largely intact there. Since full Hawaiian sovereignty has been suspended for more than a hundred years, we need to familiarize ourselves with its outlines in practical ways. What would the skin of sovereignty feel like? How would we organize and regulate our sovereign world?

To date, the manifold discussions on sovereignty have tended to divide rather than unite us. It would help to see a living example of sovereignty in action. We could practice, correct mistakes, change direction. I am concerned that without some experience of self-governance on a discrete land base, when sovereignty arrives we will be unprepared. The return of political power, while sought after, can also be a dangerous genie.

Different models of sovereignty can be established on different islands. Integrating ancestral knowledge with the dictates of modern life is a challenge we are ready for. As native people, we could soon find ourselves once again living in a sovereign land.

CITIZEN PARTICIPATION

Eight years under the anvil of Governor Linda Lingle's administration is a lesson in the wisdom of term limits. As students and parents of students learned, after conducting an eight-day protest during the 2010 legislative session against school furloughs, the governor was not interested in hearing what they had to say. Instead of using

Citizen allies Dana Naone Hall and ninety-four-year-old Mary Evanson, Sierra Club Maui Chapter chair for many years.

Photograph by Isaac Hall.

the occasion as a teaching moment, the governor was inhospitable and intractable, chiding the protestors for being underfoot in her front office, never once engaging them in dialogue.

Governor Lingle prides herself on never compromising except on her own terms. This refusal to engage openly with constituents over vexing issues has led to pitched battles and deep divisions. Perhaps the most striking feature of her tenure has been a willingness to ignore the law.

Chapter 92, Hawai'i's law on public agency meetings and records popularly known as the Sunshine Law, contains stirring language that "the people are vested with the ultimate decision-making power" in a democracy and that "opening up the governmental processes to public scrutiny and participation" is the way to protect the public's interest. Those who found their way to the governor's office were attempting to influence decision-making politely and directly for the sake of Hawai'i's students. Unhampered by the animosity between the governor and the Hawai'i State Teachers Association, they offered another plan for ending the stalemate. Many were first-time participants in government decision-making, and one parent spokeswoman told the local newspaper that everyone involved from the protestors' side "learned a lot about how government works and how to be a part of the process."

It could easily be said that governmental processes work only when they are open. Such a perspective would involve not just impartiality and fairness on the part of government decision-makers, but also what I would call a certain disinterestedness, meaning that the decision-maker is guided more by applicable laws and administrative rules than by loyalty to one party or another. Too often decisions appear to be foregone, especially when it comes to development projects or virtually any decision involving the economy. The opposite of a disinterested posture is exemplified by the dismissive response of Ted Liu, director of the Department of Business Economic Development and Tourism, to a reporter's question about the irregularities found in an audit of DBEDT: "I serve at the pleasure of Governor Linda Lingle," he said.

Hawaiʻi has a number of laws established to require a weighing of economic interests in concert with other equally valuable considerations. Economic interests are undisputedly important but are not meant to dominate decision-making.

These include the statute governing our coastal zone areas and Hawaiʻi's environmental protection law. Often these two laws work together to protect vulnerable and important coastal resources. In recent years, when the state has sought to duck environmental review, citizens have been forced to seek relief in the courts, at times with spectacular success—a notable example is the Hawaiʻi Superferry case.

The laws discussed in this section, along with Hawaiʻi's historic preservation law, are all worthy models for a Native Hawaiian entity to consider. No matter how large the land base of the eventual Hawaiian nation, it is not likely to incorporate all the land in Hawaiʻi. We must remember that any modern division, māhele, of lands will not include all culturally significant properties. Therefore our responsibility to advocate for and negotiate on behalf of these lands will continue. Endeavors of this nature will require us to work in common cause with other citizen allies who also love Hawaiʻi.

Published in *The Value of Hawaiʻi: Knowing the Past, Shaping the Future*, eds. Craig Howes and Jonathan Kay Kamakawiwoʻole Osorio (Honolulu: Published for the Biographical Research Center by the University of Hawaiʻi Press, 2010), 195–200.

Kawananakoa Tomb

51

BOARD OF LAND AND NATURAL RESOURCES MEETING
APRIL 26, 2013

The proposal of Abigail Kawananakoa to construct a tomb to house her remains is *not* a request that this board should decide in the absence of much wider discussion and consultation involving, first and foremost, the greater Hawaiian community, and the Department of Land and Natural Resource's (DLNR's) own in-house experts, including culture and history branch staff at the State Historic Preservation Division (SHPD), and the ethnography and archaeology staff available at State Parks.

Many look to Mauna 'Ala not only as a sacred burial site but also as an island of sovereignty where Ka Hae Hawai'i, the Hawaiian flag, is flown in solemn testament to the abiding hope that our nation may one day be restored. The form and shape of that restoration is a topic of lively debate among Hawaiian people, who should be afforded the courtesy of participating in decision-making on the instant request.

The staff report footnotes a 1956 opinion letter approved by an acting attorney general under the Territory of Hawaii as the legal underpinning for the assertion that jurisdiction over who can be buried at Mauna 'Ala has devolved to DLNR. At a minimum, there should be a fresh look at the legal implications of this request. The last burial occurred in 1953, sixty years ago. All of the burials—many dating to the nineteenth century—are historic burials, meaning that they are at least fifty years old or older.

A number of important laws concerning cemeteries and burial sites have been enacted in the past fifty years, which give rise to the following questions, among others.

- Is Mauna 'Ala a cemetery?
- Would the construction of a new tomb to receive the remains of Ms. Kawananakoa subject Mauna 'Ala to the jurisdiction of the Department of Health and Hawai'i Revised Statues (HRS) Chapter 441, which governs mausoleums with one or more vaults or crypts?
- With a modern interment, would Mauna 'Ala be considered an active cemetery? If so, a registered cemetery authority would be required by law.

If an Archaeological Inventory Survey is required, as would be appropriate prior to site selection (ground disturbance will be required to construct the concrete base of the tomb), and burials are identified, would these burials be treated under HRS Section (§)6E-43?

The board must ask itself what kind of precedent it would be setting and how it plans to deal with future requests.

An application consisting of a six-sentence written narrative about the project (one sentence of which is "Thank you for your consideration") is insufficient in terms of identifying the project's potential impacts.

The myriad issues that arise from the Kawananakoa request must be examined carefully. I was disheartened to see in the staff report the recommendation that the project be exempted from the preparation of an Environmental Assessment (EA) on the basis that the subject action falls within Exemption Class 3. The 21 specifically enumerated exemptions in Exemption Class 3 all contain references to parks, such as construction of enclosures for park trash containers, park picnic tables, park picnic stoves, cooking grills, and BBQs. Clearly, the subject request does not fit into any of the numbered Class 3 exemptions.

Furthermore, on the last page of the [2013] Exemption List for DLNR's Division of State Parks is the following note, which applies to all six exemption classes:

> Pursuant to HAR §11-200-8(b), all exemptions under the classes in this section are inapplicable . . . when an action that is normally insignificant in its impact on the environment may be significant in a particularly sensitive environment.

Anyone who is at all familiar with the Royal Mausoleum, even the casual visitor, cannot help but be moved by the grandeur and gravity of the place. It would be difficult to imagine a more sensitive environment. This is underscored by the fact that the Royal Mausoleum has been listed on the National Register of Historic Places since 1972 and on the Hawai'i Register of Historic Places since 1981.

Hawai'i's environmental law in HRS §343.5 states that an environmental assessment shall be required for actions that "(1) Propose the use of state . . . lands" and "(4) Propose any use within any historic site as designated in the National Register or Hawai'i Register."

It would be a serious mistake, and an offense to a sacred site, to exempt this project from the requirement for an EA. Public participation is built into the EA process, allowing agencies and all interested persons an opportunity to comment.

Given the legal uncertainties as to jurisdiction and the lack of an environmental assessment, I respectfully ask that the board deny this request or, at a minimum, defer action on this matter until required studies are prepared, including an environmental assessment and an archaeological inventory survey.

52

Introduction to Maui Showing of Act of War: The Overthrow of the Hawaiian Nation

DOCUMENTARY FILM PREMIERE 1993

Tonight's showing of *Act of War* is historic in more than one sense. The documentary traces the historic events that led to the overthrow of the lawful government of Hawai'i and the loss of Hawaiian sovereignty in 1893. The title of the documentary is taken from President Grover Cleveland's explanation to the US Congress about why he would not further the cause of the annexationists. Cleveland called the overthrow "an act of war."

The making of the documentary that you are about to see was itself a historic event. The principal consultants and scriptwriters are Hawaiian women who are leaders in the sovereignty movement. A hundred years after Lili'uokalani was deposed from her throne, Hawaiian women have come forward to reclaim the right to self-government. This is not to suggest that this passage has been in any way an easy one. The way has been fraught with obstructions, and there are many obstacles yet to be overcome.

We are living in adverse times, but this is not a lament since such times challenge us to examine ourselves and our relationship to powerful forces bent on destroying our islands and our culture. Of course, anyone who challenges the dominant economic forces is sure to be declared a "political extremist," a "radical," and "antidevelopment," as well as other far less savory labels. This characteristic labeling is part of an effort to marginalize any opposition and to deflect attention from the real issues at hand.

So it takes courage to withstand the onslaught and to be heard above the insistent cries of those who would prefer that we not be heard at all.

I am deeply indebted to Haunani-Kay Trask and, more recently but no less deeply, to Lilikalā Kameʻeleihiwa for their courage, for their scholarship, and for the aloha that is at the core of their penetrating words and actions.

Dana Naone Hall at ʻIolani Palace during the one-hundredth-year anniversary of the overthrow of the Hawaiian Kingdom.
Photograph by Masako Cordray.

Legislative Hearing on House Bill 1992 and Senate Bill 1639 Relating to a Hawaiian Congress 53

MABEL SMYTH AUDITORIUM, HONOLULU, OʻAHU

FEBRUARY 15, 1993

Good afternoon, senators and representatives. My name is Dana Naone Hall. I've come from Maui today to testify against your adoption of House Bill 1992 and Senate Bill 1639.

The bills are seriously flawed and would have the effect of foreclosing discussion on a subject that is just beginning to be initiated on a wider and much needed basis. There is tremendous pressure to pass sovereignty legislation this year, but instead of tying ourselves to a make-or-break situation in 1993, we should be encouraging full and open discussions with the ultimate goal of finding common ground. Then it would not be a matter of one group imposing its will on others. The bills before you now are not in the best interests of the Hawaiian communities.

For example, the timeline for the election of delegates, the convening of a Hawaiian congress, and the ratification of an organic document developed by the congress is extremely compressed. All of this major work will take place in approximately six months. After a 100-year suspension of our sovereign power, these bills would direct the formation of a sovereign entity in half a year.

There are many, many people who are learning only this year the historical facts of the overthrow. It would be fair to say that the great majority of Hawaiians in this state do not have a clear idea of what sovereignty is and what form it should take for our people. If we want to involve people in an elective process of this magnitude, then we have a duty to make sure that they are educated about the particulars.

I realize that some groups have been actively working to educate and inform the Hawaiian communities, but that outreach has not yet penetrated far enough. On Maui, the Office of Hawaiian Affairs (OHA) trustee for our island, to my knowledge has never held a meeting to discuss sovereignty issues and certainly has not taken the time to inform us of the legislation that has been submitted this session. Last year some prominent members of Ka Lāhui Hawai'i came to Maui to inform an enthusiastic crowd of 300 about sovereignty. That's a beginning, and we need more of it. Attempts must be made to reach the other 23,000 Hawaiians who live in Maui County alone.

More in the way of vigorous public debates, among other forums, must take place on each of the islands. By this I mean that members of the contesting sovereignty groups should be on the same panels and appear in the same forums.

There's no overwhelming reason why a decision to determine the actual course of sovereignty for us all cannot be delayed for a year while education and coming together take place. This is the hope and promise of government—the kind of government we envision. I might add that at these same forums disclosure can be made about OHA's continuing negotiations with the state regarding the ceded lands trust.

We haven't had the chance to find our common ground, our common foundation. I'm not here today as a member of a particular partisan group, although I am a member of Native Hawaiian organizations on Maui. Somehow we must find a way to overcome our partisan interests. It can be done.

Just such a coming together was accomplished, on a more limited basis, when a revision to Hawai'i Revised Statutes Chapter 6E, Hawai'i's historic preservation law, was approved by the legislature in 1990. The revision to 6E involved the establishment of island burial councils whose primary jurisdiction is the protection and general treatment of Native Hawaiian burials. As you recall, this change in the law was brought about by the controversy at Honokahua and the disinterment of nearly 1,000 Native Hawaiian burials that occurred there.

A burial bill submitted to the 1989 legislature did not win passage. Following that failure, a working group involving and including Native Hawaiian representatives of all of the populated islands—as well as OHA and other interested parties—got together and over the course of numerous meetings developed a much better and stronger piece of legislation. This bill, as I stated earlier, was passed in 1990.

The year between the two bills proved to be critical. The same period would be appropriate here. It may be that in the intervening year a consensus will develop that the convening of a Hawaiian congress is not the best means for establishing a sovereign nation.

If, however, a congress of some kind is convened, then I strongly object to the entire process as outlined in the current legislation. The membership of the congress as proposed would unduly favor O'ahu residents. Congressional membership based on population is not the only way to determine membership and in this case is not the right way.

Even on the basis as proposed by the Senate and House bills, membership distribution is not strictly based on population. Using the figures from the 1991 State of Hawaii Data Book (the 1992 Data Book has not yet been published), the City and County of Honolulu has approximately 68% of the Hawaiian and part-Hawaiian population (these are the categories in the Data Book, not mine); Hawai'i County 14%; Kaua'i 5%; and Maui County 12%. This does not exactly comport with the delegate distribution in the OHA bill.

It appears that several additional delegates were allotted to the Big Island. Why is that? True, the county of Hawai'i is comprised of approximately 63% of the total land area in the state. Then again, Maui County has 18% of the land area but only 12 delegates, while O'ahu with only 9% of the land area garners 66 delegates. Kaua'i County with approximately the same land area as O'ahu has only 6 delegates, one of which may be claimed by Ni'ihau.

It would be far more appropriate to determine delegate distribution on the land base involved. If, for instance, the majority of ceded lands and Hawaiian Home Lands are located on the Neighbor Islands, is it just and fair to allow O'ahu delegates to have an automatic 66% majority in the proposed congress?

Equal numbers of delegates from each of the four counties may be more just and equitable. Why should O'ahu decide for Hawai'i, Hawai'i for Maui, or Maui for Kaua'i? Recognizing the discrete and fundamental differences that exist between the islands and giving each island group an equal footing would be better than the skewed membership now under consideration.

This brings me to another concern. Why is the OHA voter list to be used for both the election of delegates and the ratification of any subsequent document? The overwhelming majority of Hawaiians in Hawai'i, more than 216,000, are not OHA voters, and a significant number will not register as OHA voters because of their deep distrust of OHA. I am an OHA voter but I feel that the process will be unduly tainted and perhaps even predetermined if the OHA voter list is used.

To assure a free and open election, a separate registration process should be developed. Not everyone who claims Hawaiian blood supports sovereignty; I'm sure that this is the case among a number of OHA voters as well as non-OHA voting Hawaiians. With a separate and neutral registration, those who truly have an interest in reestablishing sovereign powers to the Hawaiian people would be participating in the decision-making.

I don't expect the legislators to agree with everything I've said, but in pointing out some of my concerns, I hope that it gives you an idea of the depth and complexity of the decision you will make. May I suggest that it is not the place of OHA to come before you to seek approval of sovereignty bills that have not had the benefit of full disclosure to the very beneficiaries in whose name this legislation is being proposed. The movement should come from the land through the people themselves, and not from nine OHA trustees who represent less than the majority of Hawaiians in Hawai'i.

The problem with the OHA bills is that the substance is yoked to the form, which, in turn, is dictated by certain anniversaries. The congress shall convene this year on the anniversary of Queen Lili'uokalani's birthday, September 2, 1838. Ratification of the organic document is to be completed no later than January 17, 1994, the 101st year anniversary of the overthrow. This must have influenced the decision to set the delegate number at 101. If this whole process is pushed forward one year, with ratification occurring in 1995 rather than 1994, and the delegate number increases to 102, what would be the harm?

Comments on the Advance Notice of Proposed Rule-Making on Procedures for Reestablishing a Government-to-Government Relationship with the Native Hawaiian Community 54

THE DEPARTMENT OF THE INTERIOR,
OFFICE OF THE SECRETARY
REGULATION IDENTIFIER NUMBER 1090-AB05
AUGUST 14, 2014

The pain of the overthrow and subsequent annexation of our islands still reverberates today, as has been made eloquently evident in numerous hearings held in Hawaiʻi by the Department of the Interior in late June and early July. It may be helpful to reflect on two overarching matters from the past: the decimation of the ʻŌiwi population from foreign diseases and epidemics, and the Māhele, which destroyed the traditional land tenure system—replacing it with a Western model of private property ownership. Both proved disastrous for Kanaka Maoli.

Embedded in this history is the protection and encouragement American missionaries received from high-ranking Aliʻi after they arrived in 1820. Thirty years later, and a month before the passage of the Kuleana Act of 1850, which confirmed the rights of the Makaʻāinana to land ownership, foreigners who had sworn no allegiance to the Hawaiian government were allowed by the legislature to buy and sell land. Haole who had become Hawaiian citizens, and were often dual citizens, already enjoyed this privilege.

By the mid-1860s sugar was the king of commerce, and the effects of the last 150 years of displacement from the land, and the diversion and wasting of our precious water, continue to this day.

This brief reflection on the past is meant only to suggest that political power had been shifting long before the illegal overthrow (some of the actions native leaders took to protect the Hawaiian Kingdom from the interference of other governments had the opposite effect).

Our sovereignty is inherent, but how is it expressed in practical terms? Rhetorical statements to the contrary, saying so by itself doesn't make it so. Can we learn from the past and move forward, or do we continue to cry out in sorrow and anger?

Since the 1970s, Native Hawaiians have achieved notable victories (some of which I have contributed to). More recently, however, the political climate has changed and the hard-won recognition of fundamental Native Hawaiian rights is under attack. Primarily for this reason, I am in favor of the proposed federal rule-making process. This is in the nature of an emergency procedure, which must not foreclose the option of international redress.

We cannot wait any longer; our kahua is being chipped away as we delay engaging in an open discussion. Let our differences enliven the debate rather than divide us. Most of all, let us not lose our essential compassion and connection to one another as ʻŌiwi. Aloha.

Coda: Opening the Gates

55

JUNE 24, 2016

In February of this year, approximately eighty-eight unelected individuals met to draft a governing document to create a Native Hawaiian government. By month's end the majority of the group voted to approve the draft constitution. However, four months later this document has not been presented to the general Native Hawaiian populace for review and comment hearings, let alone ratification.

Crafted behind closed doors (or, in this case, the closed gates of the ironically named Royal Hawaiian Golf Club), the document cannot be legitimized by a vote of the people. This hurried attempt was in response to the issuance of an injunction by the US Supreme Court halting an earlier iteration of the process to elect delegates who would convene to develop a governance document.

Neither process was designed to fairly represent the Hawaiian people and their lands. A timeline and apportionment of delegates was simply announced by an organization called Naʻi Aupuni. On its own, Naʻi Aupuni determined that there would be 40 elected delegates apportioned "based on the current geographic distribution of population within the Roll Commission's current registry."

Aside from the fact that the legitimacy of the Roll Commission has been called into question, the apportionment favors Oʻahu with 20 of the 40 delegates or 50%. Combined with the 7 delegates (17.5%)

allotted to out-of-state Hawaiians, these two groups represent nearly 70% of the total delegates (67.5%), while the six other inhabited Hawaiian islands (Hawai'i, Maui, Moloka'i, Lāna'i, Kaua'i, and Ni'ihau) together are to be represented by 13 delegates (32.5%). Clearly there are other, fairer, more representative ways of designating delegates.

This end note is a plea for a visibly inclusive process, which will require discipline on the part of both sides of the ongoing debate: one side cannot simply impose its will on the other. It may be better to begin by treating each island as an autonomous unit, holding its own internal debate and discussion, before convening any larger 'aha. There are sure to be common concerns, but the priority these concerns are given, and the ways in which they can be addressed, are likely to be as diverse as the islands themselves. Let's open the gates and talk.

Hoʻi hou i Mākena.

Photograph by Dana Naone Hall.

A Poetry of Place

56

PRESENTATION TO FIRST NATIONS
FUTURES PROGRAM FELLOWS
JANUARY 12, 2015

I grew up in Kāne'ohe at the foot of the Ko'olau mountains, whose charged, green presence shaped and informed my early years. Another powerful influence was the public library built sometime in the late 1950s. At that time, in our very small, rural town, I could see, from the hill we lived on, the roof of the library—that magical storehouse of the imagination. A recurrent happy thought was of being in a room with stacks of all the books I had read, which would continue to grow over time.

I wrote my first poem as a freshman at the Kamehameha School for Girls (in the last year that Kamehameha had an all-girls' school). The subject of the poem was Venice, assigned by our English teacher who held us all in check—if not fear—with her erect posture and formidable diction. I was surprised to find that my poem had been one of the ones chosen to be printed in a little year-end booklet. I can still remember the sibilant sounds I managed to cram into the poem's last line.

Those experiences of the power of place and the joy and invention of the imagination are still sources of my political and public life today, with much learned along the way.

In the 1970s, the movement to stop the bombing on Kaho'olawe sent out wide ripples and caused many of us to question what was happening to our islands. The Hawaiian Renaissance woke people up, and Waiāhole and Waikāne, Kalama Valley, and Kahoʻolawe were among the first calls to action. Kūpuna gravity and humor, and youthful idealism and energy, bound together by grassroots organizing, were in full display.

As a people we were reminded that while we may look at the past 200 and more years since Western contact through a Hawaiian prism, we must also examine the economic forces that shaped that history and continue to dictate much of what happens to this day.

My first full-scale engagement on Maui occurred in the mid-1980s over Seibu Corporation's attempt to close a portion of the old Mākena coastal road in order to consolidate its mauka and makai lands for hotel and resort uses, essentially privatizing a beautiful white sand beach at Maluaka. This strategy of closing coastal roads had been employed first at Kāʻanapali and then at Wailea, where old roads that followed the shore were replaced by highways located a considerable distance inland. Hotels sprouted below the new highways on land that now afforded unrestricted access for hotel guests to many of Maui's best beaches, while simultaneously restricting and even eliminating access by the public and Native Hawaiians.

The diminishment and loss of access at Kāʻanapali and Wailea reverberated when Seibu sought the same accommodation. What many of us didn't realize was that, in terms of land use decision-making, we were at least a decade too late. We were protesting a land use policy decision made in the 1970s when there was no public awareness and little participation, and summarily incorporated into a draft community plan for the Kīhei-Mākena region. The struggle over the provision to close a portion of the old Mākena Road brought together Native Hawaiians, who formed a group that still exists today, called Hui Alanui o Mākena. I am a member of the Hui, and my husband Isaac Hall, in the course of the controversy, filed six lawsuits on behalf of the Hui.

It was an exciting time, full of learning and commitment, with the odds greatly stacked against us. Even so, there was a strong desire to maintain a connection to and presence in the place—sustained by our belief that the old road followed the alignment of the Pi'ilani Trail, which had evolved over time to become the old road.

Seibu hired a consultant from another island who testified before the county council that he had walked the road and declared that there was no mana. On the other hand, Hui Alanui kupuna Aunty Alice Kuloloio said the road was alive and that it was breathing.

During this time, I visited the Museum of the American Indian in Lower Manhattan and saw a black-and-white photo of pueblo dwellers gathering for a ceremonial dance (elders, parents, and children). The photo was mounted on a semicircular half wall so that the viewer stood in the opening in the circle as a participant in the scene and not merely as an observer. This feeling was reinforced by the exhibit's caption:

> Traditions fluctuate.
> They stop and start,
> they disappear and reappear again—
> they are even neglected.
> but you can always return to them
> at any point in the circle.

The words underscored for me the ability to continue traditions and practices even if they disappear for a time or evolve over time.

After three years of holding off Seibu, the conflict took an unexpected turn. In an appearance before a Maui Circuit Court judge on one of the Hui's pending lawsuits, instead of ruling on the merits of the case, the judge ordered Seibu and the Hui to mediate. He proceeded to appoint former Maui Mayor Elmer Cravalho, a savvy and seasoned politician, as the mediator.

Mayor Cravalho traveled to Japan after discussions with us to meet directly with the head of Seibu, Yoshiaki Tsutsumi—the owner of Seibu Railway and the international Prince Hotel chain, among other interests. *Forbes* magazine had recently named him the richest man in the world. The result was an unprecedented settlement agreement. In exchange for closing a 1,100-foot-long section of road to vehicular access, the 20-foot-wide road would remain open for unrestricted pedestrian access. The Hui designed the 20-foot-wide trail access to differentiate it from the adjoining hotel property.

Parks at both the north and south ends of the 1,100-foot section were agreed to, along with ample parking for beachgoers and fishermen. There were other considerations as well, including a commitment by Seibu, and binding on its successors-in-interest, not to seek or support any further closures of Mākena Road. The Hui also received 3 acres of land. Most important, something of the past would be preserved to give life to future endeavors in unforeseen ways.

As the Mākena Road issue was working its way toward resolution, my husband and I became aware by chance, while sitting in the last Maui County Planning Commission meeting of 1986, that another portion of the Pi‘ilani trail had been found at Honokahua where Maui Land and Pineapple Company, through its subsidiary Kapalua Land Company, planned to build a hotel. We also learned that burials had been identified at the proposed hotel site. This began another three-year battle to protect the Honokahua Burial Site. I won't go into great detail here; I have written about this subject elsewhere, and these sources are readily available.

I believe that our work as the Hui involving Mākena Road, and its prehistoric beginnings as part of a trail that circled the island of Maui, led us to Honokahua. Once there we encountered a situation that we could not turn away from.

When the administrative proceedings had been exhausted and the disinterment began in August 1987, I made the hour-and-a-half drive each way typically twice a week until the digging was stopped by Governor John Waihe‘e in December 1988. It took most of 1989 to redo agreements between variously the Office of Hawaiian Affairs, the state of Hawai‘i, Kapalua Land Company, and the Hui, to obtain settlement funds from the Hawai‘i State Legislature, and to amend county permits.

The legislature allocated $6 million, with $5.5 million of that sum to be paid to Kapalua Land Company for planning and design, and other preconstruction costs, including a burgeoning bill for archaeological work. Kapalua Land's President Colin Cameron characterized the payment as making the company whole. (Officially, the payment was for a conservation easement in favor of the state of Hawai'i.) The remaining half million would be used for reinterment costs. A hālau kapa was established to make kapa for wrapping the iwi of more than a thousand individuals. And a team of men was assembled to wrap the iwi. I worked with Maui Land and Pineapple Vice President Richard Cameron to coordinate and pay the women and men, but accepted no money for myself. Nor have I ever been in the Ritz-Carlton, Kapalua, hotel. These actions are my continuing ho'okupu to the kūpuna buried there.

Because we chose to bear witness to Honokahua out of aloha for the iwi kupuna, eventually justice was done. Or as American theologian and ethicist Reinhold Niebuhr wrote, "Love is the motive, but justice is the instrument." This quote closely expresses my point of view.

Another reflection: It often seemed that one burning issue led to another like one torch lighting the next before its flame is extinguished.

While we were undergoing the pain of Honokahua, I had to have my "wisdom" teeth pulled. A friend of mine had had the procedure done and highly recommended laughing gas. She said she felt carefree and ebullient the entire time. Unfortunately, the laughing gas had the opposite effect on me. I was miserable and identified the tooth pulling with the iwi being extracted from their resting places. I vowed to do everything in my power to prevent another large-scale sand dune burial excavation. The chance to fulfill this vow came soon enough.

Out of tragic circumstances at Honokahua arose awareness of the need to protect prehistoric burials, which are mostly unmarked on the surface, unlike the marked burials found in cemeteries or other historic contexts. Many of these unmarked burials repose in sand dunes. Honokahua provided the impetus for the creation of Hawai'i's burial law, Hawai'i Revised Statutes Section 6E-43, an entirely new section of our state's historic preservation law.

In the early 1990s, Sokan, a Japanese corporation, planned to build an 18-hole golf course and expansive clubhouse on coastal land in Waiheʻe, Maui. A large portion of the parcel proposed for development contained an inland sand dune nearly 300 feet high in elevation. Five historic cemeteries were arrayed along the top and western slope of the dune, while the dune itself likely contained higher numbers of precontact burials than at Honokahua. Bordered on the north by Waiheʻe Stream, the shoreline land between the eastern foot of the dune and the ocean once featured an inland fishpond (now a wetland), an ancient village, and at least three heiau—one of which is still visible today. What a treasure trove it is. I thought often that the only thing missing is Hawaiian people.

On the eve of the commencement of contested case proceedings regarding a Special Management Area permit for the golf course, Sokan's attorney requested an indefinite continuance. The practice of trading golf course memberships on the Japanese stock market and selling memberships to finance the construction of new golf courses was no longer viable. The Japanese economic bubble had burst, opening the way for the eventual acquisition of this precious land by the Maui Coastal Land Trust, which has since become a part of the Hawaiian Islands Land Trust.

I sometimes worried about the passage of kūpuna who provided such a vital link to the past—Aunty Alice, Uncle Eddie Chang, Kahu David Kaʻalakea. Then it occurred to me that the land is our teacher, too. In saying this I acknowledge that I am neither a farmer (although I have been an occasional gardener) nor a fisherman.

However, I have participated in hundreds of site visits to archaeological and cultural sites. In addition, I have read (and often commented on) scores of archaeological and burial reports and plans. Because of this familiarity I look at sand dunes differently even when they are no longer physically present on the surface—as is the case with the Ward Villages project, where concentrations of intact burials were identified under a parking area, in the sandy matrix of a backshore dune located mauka of Ala Moana Boulevard. The remnant dune and the burials it contained had survived repeated episodes of historic disturbance, including fill brought into the area to create fast land for urban development. Their continued existence, like the rock walls of an ancient house site or subsurface cultural layers full of midden and interspersed with hearths, is a clear and positive reminder that ka poʻe kahiko were survivors and so are we.

A final note: All around us, wherever we live, land is being changed beyond recognition. I mentioned earlier that the Hui had received 3 acres of land in the ahupuaʻa of Moʻoloa as part of the settlement agreement with Seibu. For years the land, full of kiawe and other thorny alien plant species, lay unattended. Our first attempt at development resulted in plans for a structure that would have taken all of our funds and produced a building that mimicked the high-end developments of present-day Wailea and Mākena, albeit on a much smaller scale.

I woke up one morning and realized that our plans were all wrong and that the emphasis should be on bringing life back to the land as a Hawaiian place; any structure would be ancillary to that purpose. Even though we were halfway through the building permit process, we scrapped those plans and started again. Our ʻāina at Moʻoloa (for which we are temporary stewards) is moving in the opposite direction from the rest of the built environment around it. It is evolving toward something more recognizable but not a strict facsimile of the past. Less Proust's *Remembrance of Things Past* and more like Michael J. Fox in *Back to the Future*.

In my thinking, traditions are not monolithic. They must be continually refreshed at the roots by the present and next generations. This is your challenge and birthright as ʻŌiwi in the twenty-first century.

Keoneʻōʻio Fishpond

57

If you do not see
how those here raised
the soft-nosed needlefish,
Look again.

GLOSSARY

Ae'o. Hawaiian stilt (*Himantopus mexicanus knudseni*).
'Aha. Assembly, meeting.
'Āhinahina. The Haleakalā silversword (*Argyroxiphium sandwicense* subsp. *macrocephalum*).
Ahu. Altar, shrine.
Ahupua'a. Land division generally extending from uplands to the sea.
'Āina. Land.
'Āina momona. Rich and fertile land.
Akule. Big-eyed scad (*Selar crumenophthalmus*), a favorite fish for drying.
Ala. Path. To awaken.
'Alae ke'oke'o. Hawaiian coot (*Fulica alai*).
Alaloa. Main road or trail, belt road.
Alanui. Road or trail, highway, thoroughfare.
Ali'i. Chief, chiefess.
Aloha. Love, compassion; greeting.
Aloha ahiahi. Good evening.
Aloha 'āina. Love of the land, patriotism.
'Auwai. Irrigation ditch, canal.
'Aumakua. Family god, deified ancestor.
'Aumākua. Plural of 'aumakua.
'Āwikiwiki. Endemic perennial climber (*Canavalia hawaiiensis*).

Ea. Sovereignty. Life, air, breath.

Ha'aheo. Proud.
Hae Hawai'i. Hawaiian flag.
Hālau kapa. Structure or specific place where kapa is made.
Hale. House, building.
Hao. Endemic small tree (*Rauvolfia mauiensis*).
Haole. Caucasian, foreigner.
Heiau. Traditional place of worship.
Hewa. Offense, wrong.
Hinahina. Indigenous prostrate shrub (*Heliotropium anomalum*) with sweetly fragrant flowers.
Hō'ailona. Sign, portent.
Ho'okupu. Ceremonial offering, tribute.
Ho'opono. To make right.
Ho'oponopono. Traditional spiritually based process that engages family members in righting negative actions, thoughts, and feelings in order to restore harmonious relationships.
Hui. Organization, association, group.
Hukilau. To fish with a seine net.

'Ili. Subdivision of an ahupua'a.
'Ili'ili. Waterworn pebble, small stone.
Imu. Underground oven.
Iwi. Bones.
Iwi kupuna. Ancestral bones.

Kahu. Guardian, honored keeper, pastor of a church.
Kahua. Foundation, base.
Kalo. Taro (*Colocasia esculenta*), a Polynesian introduction, and the physical and spiritual core of Hawaiian life.

Kanaka Maoli. Native Hawaiian.
Kanaka ʻŌiwi. Native Hawaiian.
Kāne. God of creation, fresh water, and agriculture, embodied in the taro plant. Also means "man."
Kapa. Tapa, bark cloth.
Kiaʻāina. Governor.
Kiawe. Algaroba tree (*Prosopis pallida*) introduced to Hawaiʻi in 1828.
Koʻa. Fishing shrine.
Kokiʻo. Endemic hibiscus with fragrant flowers.
Koloa maoli. Hawaiian duck (*Anas wyvilliana*).
Kolomona. Indigenous shrub (*Senna gaudichaudii*).
Konohiki. Headman or woman of an ahupuaʻa.
Kūkini. Runner, swift messenger.
Kukui. Candlenut tree (*Aleurites moluccana*), a symbol of enlightenment.
Kulāiwi. Native land, homeland.
Kuleana. Small piece of property.
Kuleana Act. The 1850 act authorized the Land Commission to award fee-simple title to native tenants.
Kupuna. Grandparent, relative of grandparent's generation, ancestor.
Kūpuna. Plural of kupuna.
Kūʻula. Stone god used to attract fish.

Lāhui. Nation, race, people.
Lāhui Hawaiʻi. Hawaiian Nation, Hawaiian Race.
Lehua. Flower of the endemic ʻōhiʻa tree (*Metrosideros polymorpha*); also the tree itself (figuaratively, a warrior).
Lei niho palaoa. Hook-shaped pendant worn only by aliʻi.
Lei ʻōpuʻu. Bud-shaped ornament worn by aliʻi.
Limu. Algae, seaweed.
Limu kala. Common seaweed (*Sargassum echinocarpum*) used in certain ceremonies.
Loʻi. Irrigated terrace or paddy.
Loʻi kalo. Irrigated paddy or terrace for taro cultivation.
Loko iʻa. Fishpond.
Loulu. Endemic fan palm (*Pritchardia*).
Lūʻau. Hawaiian feast.

Māhele. Historical 1848 event that transformed the Hawaiian system of land tenure from traditional communal use to private ownership.
Makaʻāinana. Commoners, people in general, people who tend the land.
Makahiki. Traditional festival held for about four months, beginning around October, during which time war was prohibited.
Makai. Toward the sea.
Mālama ʻāina. Caring for the land.
Malo. Loin cloth.
Mana. Spiritual power.
Manō. Sharks, generally; some sharks were ʻaumakua.
Mauka. Toward the mountains.
Moe loa. Eternal rest.
Moepū. Funerary objects.
Moku. District, island, section.
Moʻo. Lizard; water spirit.
Moʻolelo. History, story.

Naio. Indigenous tree (*Myoporum sandwicense*) whose wood, when burned, smelled like sandalwood.
Nāulu. Name of a rain cloud or rain shower associated with Haleakalā and Kahoʻolawe.
Naupaka. Endemic and indigenous shrub species (*Scaevola*).
Nehe. Endemic shrubs and herbs (*Lipochaeta* spp.)

Noni. Indian mulberry (*Morinda citrifolia*), a Polynesian introduction. Hawaiians used different parts of the plant for dyes and medicine.

ʻŌhiʻa. Endemic tree ʻōhiʻa lehua (*Metrosideros polymorpha*).
ʻŌʻio. Bonefish (*Albula vulpes*).
ʻŌiwi. Native.
Oli. Chant.
One hānau. Land of one's birth (literally, "birth sands").
ʻOpihi. Limpet.

Paʻa. Secure, steadfast.
Pahu. Drum.
Pili. Indigenous grass (*Heteropogon contortus*) used for thatching.
Pipipi. Small ocean mollusk (*Theodoxus neglectus*).
Poʻe. People.
Poʻe Hawaiʻi. Hawaiian people.
Poʻe kahiko. People of old.
Pōhaku. Rock, stone.
Poi. Hawaiian staple food made from cooked and pounded taro.
Pono. Good, just, righteous, balanced.
Popo. Grandmother (Chinese term).
Pueo. Hawaiian short-eared owl (*Asio flammeus sandwichensis*).
Pūneʻe. Day bed, couch.
Puʻu. Hill.

Tūtū. Grandparent, relative, or close friend of grandparent's generation.

Uhu. Parrotfish, including *Scarus perspicillatus*, a favorite of Hawaiians especially when eaten raw.
Ulua. Certain species of crevally, jackfish (Carangidae).

Wahi pana. Sacred place, legendary or storied place.

REFERENCES

Barrère, Dorothy B. 1994. *The King's Mahele: The Awardees and Their Lands*. Volcano, Hawai'i: Dorothy B. Barrère.

Berdeshevsky, Margo. 1991. Excerpts from "A Hawaiian Woman and a Warrior," an interview with Dana Naone Hall. *Island Currents*, February, 6–7.

Bettger, Lyle. April 28, 1992. Letter to the editor. *Maui News*.

Boudreau, Martin, Jack Henry, Paul H. Rosendahl, and Patricia Kalima. 1992. *Additional Inventory Survey Burial Findings, Waihee Golf Club*. Hilo: Paul H. Rosendahl.

Boudreau, Martin, and Peter M. Jensen. 1992. *Additional Inventory Survey Non-Burial Findings*. Hilo: Paul H. Rosendahl.

Dega, Michael, and Rachel Hoerman. 2009. *Preservation Component of a Burial Treatment Plan for Multiple Burials Discovered on a 18,106 Square Foot Parcel in Wainiha Ahupua'a, Halele'a District, Island of Kaua'i, Hawai'i*. Honolulu: Scientific Consultant Services.

Dega, Michael, Rachel Hoerman, Donna Schefcheck, and Piphal Heng. 2008. *An Archaeological Inventory Survey of a 15,667 Square Foot Parcel in Wainiha Ahupua'a, Halele'a District, Island of Kaua'i, Hawai'i*. Honolulu: Scientific Consultant Services.

Donham, Theresa K. 1989. *Archaeological Inventory Survey, Proposed Waihee Golf Club Project Area, Lands of Waihee and Waiehu, Wailuku District, Island of Maui, TMK:3-2-10, 12*. Hilo: Paul H. Rosendahl.

Donham, Theresa K. 1992. *Additional Archaeological Subsurface Testing, Proposed Waihee Golf Club Project Area, Lands of Waihee and Waiehu, Wailuku District, Island of Maui, TMK:3-2-10:1*. Hilo: Paul H. Rosendahl.

Dye, Bob. 2000. "Bishop Estate's First Trustees Played Key Role in Overthrow." *Honolulu Advertiser*, opinion, March 12. http://thehonoluluadvertiser.com/2000/Mar/12/opinion6.html.

Editorial, "Ho'okipa's Beauty Can Be Improved." 1988. *Maui News*, March 4.

Hammatt, Hallett H., and David Shideler. 2006. *Archaeological Monitoring Plan for the Kawaiaha'o Church Ancillary Facilities Project, Kawaiaha'o, Kona District, O'ahu, TMK [1] 1-2-1-032:017*. Kailua: Cultural Surveys Hawai'i.

Handy, E. S. Craighill, and Elizabeth Green Handy, with the collaboration of Mary Kawena Pukui. 1972. *Native Planters in Old Hawaii*. Honolulu: Bishop Museum Press.

Handy, E. S. Craighill, and Mary Kawena Pukui. 1989. *The Polynesian Family System in Ka-ʻu, Hawaiʻi*. Rutland and Tokyo: Tuttle.

Hedani, Wayne. 1992. Letter to the editor. *Maui News*, May 13.

Kamakau, Samuel Manaiakalani. 1992A. *Ruling Chiefs of Hawaii*. Honolulu: Kamehameha Schools Press.

Kamakau, Samuel Manaiakalani. 1992B. *The Works of the People of Old*. Honolulu: Bishop Museum Press.

Kameʻeleihiwa, Lilikalā. 1992. *Native Land and Foreign Desires: Pehea Lā E Pono Ai?* Honolulu: Bishop Museum Press.

Kehler, Annalise. June 4, 2015. Meeting of the Maui County Cultural Resources Commission. The minutes for this meeting are available online at http://www.co.maui.hi.us/ArchiveCenter/ViewFile/Item/20875.

Lydgate, J. M. 1912. "Affairs of the Wainiha Hui," *Hawaiian Almanac and Annual for 1913*, pp. 125–37. Honolulu: Thos. G. Thrum.

Merry, Sally Engle. 2000. *Colonizing Hawaiʻi: The Cultural Power of Law*. Princeton: Princeton University Press.

Naone Hall, Dana. 1992. "INCOMING! Maui's Multi-Million Dollar Airport Expansion Doesn't Make Sense." *Honolulu Weekly*, January 1.

Naone Hall, Dana. 2013. "The Road to Cultural Justice." *Society for American Archaeology Record* 13 (1): 37–39.

O'Hare, Constance. 2005. *Background Information in Support of Subsurface Testing, Monitoring and Burial Treatment Plans for the Kawaiahaʻo Church Ancillary Facility Project, Honolulu Ahupuaʻa, Kawaiahaʻo ʻIli, Kona District, Island of Oʻahu*. Kailua: Cultural Surveys Hawaiʻi.

Pukui, Mary Kawena. 1983. *ʻŌlelo Noʻeau*. Honolulu: Bishop Museum Press.

Pukui, Mary Kawena, and Samuel H. Elbert. 1986. *Hawaiian Dictionary*. Honolulu: University of Hawaiʻi Press.

State of Hawaii Data Book: A Statistical Abstract. 1991. Honolulu: Department of Business, Economic Development, and Tourism.

Tulchin, Jon, and Hallett H. Hammatt. 2006. *An Archaeological Subsurface Investigation at Kawaiahaʻo Church Cemetery, Honolulu Ahupuaʻa, Kona District, Island of Oʻahu TMK: (1) 2-1-032:016 and 017*. Kailua: Cultural Surveys Hawaiʻi, Inc.

INDEX

Page numbers in italic refer to illustrations